Air Mail

ABOUT THE AUTHOR

The day after Terry Ravenscroft threw in his mundane factory job to become a TV scriptwriter, he was involved in a car accident that left him unable to turn his head. Since then, he has never looked back. Before they took him away, he wrote scripts for Les Dawson, *The Two Ronnies*, Morecambe and Wise, *Alas Smith and Jones*, *Not the Nine O'Clock News*, Dave Allen, Frankie Howerd, Ken Dodd, Roy Hudd, Hale and Pace, and quite a few others. He also wrote many episodes of the situation comedy *Terry and June*, and the award-winning BBC Radio series *Star Terk Two*.

His other books include the novel *Football Crazy* (2006).

He has a website at www.topcomedy.co.uk.

Air Mail

Letters from the world's most troublesome passenger

**Terry
Ravenscroft**

Michael O'Mara Books Limited

First published in Great Britain in a general edition in 2007 by
Michael O'Mara Books Limited
9 Lion Yard
Tremadoc Road
London SW4 7NQ

A CIP catalogue record for this book is available from the British Library.

ISBN: 978-1-84317-279-6

3 5 7 9 10 8 6 4 2

Printed and bound in Great Britain by Cox & Wyman, Reading, Berks

www.mombooks.com

ACKNOWLEDGEMENTS

T Ravenscroft (Mr) would like to thank all the airlines and airline staff who replied to his letters, at times with patience above and beyond the call of duty, and without whom this book would not have been possible.

The Elms
Wenter Road
New Mills
High Peak
Derbyshire

Air 2000 Ltd
Oakdale Broadfield Park   4th March
Crawley
West Sussex
RH11 9RT

Dear Air 2000

I recently had the pleasure of flying for the very first time. I've always been afraid to up until now, but I finally plucked up courage. I am certainly glad that I did, and for two reasons. One, it wasn't half so bad an experience as I had imagined it would be, and two, I had my first meal on an aeroplane. Why all the jokes about airline food? The fare we were served by Air 2000 on our flights down to Lanzarote and back was quite excellent, and I speak as a man who knows good food, eating as I do at least five ready-to-heat-up-in-the-microwave or boil-in-the-bag meals a week. Both the turkey and stuffing going down and the lasagne coming back were quite mouth-watering. Nor could I fault the starters and desserts, although it must be said that the couple seated next to me detected a 'soapy' taste in the trifle, although if you ask me it was their imagination, because it certainly tasted all right to me.

Is it possible to buy your meals? If so, could you please reply, with details of any other meals you do, your price list, and any discounts you allow for quantity.

Thanking you in anticipation.

Yours faithfully

T Ravenscroft (Mr)

AIR 2000

Air 2000 Limited Oakdale Broadfield Park Brighton Road Crawley West Sussex RH11 9RT Telephone : 0293 518966
Telex: 878434 Answerback AIRTWO G Facsimile: 0293 522927

Ref; PM/LAB

15 March

Mr T Ravenscroft
The Elms
Wenter Road
New Mills
High Peak
Derbyshire

Dear Mr Ravenscroft

I am in receipt of your letter dated 4 March, and would like to take this opportunity to thank you for your kind comments with regards to the catering provided on board your recent flights with us, and I am pleased to note that you enjoyed the meals.

However, I regret that these meals are not available for re-sale, so I am afraid you will have to continue to use your usual sources. Never-the-less, we would be very pleased to welcome you on board again in the near future, to sample the refreshments within our service once again.

Yours sincerely

Peter Malden
Associate Director – Inflight Services

Company Registration No: 1966273 (England) Registered Office: Oakdale Broadfield Park Brighton Road Crawley West Sussex RH11 9RT

Peter Malden
Associate Director
Air 2000 Ltd
Oakdale Broadfield Park
Crawley
West Sussex
RH11 9RT

The Elms
Wenter Road
New Mills
High Peak
Derbyshire

19th March

Dear Mr Malden

What absolutely marvellous news! It was quite obvious when I travelled with you that Air 2000 is generous – after all your stewardess gave me a Mint Imperial both ways – but I never thought for one moment that your generosity would extend to your offering me a free trip to sample your mouth-watering food again!

You didn't mention in your letter which airport your aeroplane would be flying from, or is the choice up to me? If so, Florida would seem to be a popular destination nowadays and would be most acceptable.

Can I make a request? Is it possible to have something other than the lasagne I had coming back when I flew with you to Lanzarote? Not of course that yours wasn't anything but exceptional – I swear I could still taste it two days later – but if I have it again I might be missing out on another of your culinary delights. For all I know your chefs may be quite ambitious, and if they can perform such breathtaking feats with a humble dish like lasagne I shudder to think what they could do to a *magret de canard aux baies de cassis*.

I would prefer to fly on the morning of the 14th of April from Manchester Airport, so if I don't hear from you before then I will assume that this is fine with you, and will present myself at your check-in desk at 9 a.m. precisely.

Yours sincerely

T Ravenscroft (Mr)

P.S. I think you are missing a great opportunity in not making your meals available for re-sale. You have far less faith in them than I have, because I remain convinced that if you were to make them available to the general public you would make far more money than you will ever make flying aeroplanes.

Air 2000 Limited Oakdale Broadfield Park Brighton Road Crawley West Sussex RH11 9RT Telephone : 0293 518966
Telex: 878434 Answerback AIRTWO G Facsimile: 0293 522927

Ref; PM/BIM

8 April

Mr T Ravenscroft
The Elms
Wenter Road
New Mills
High Peak
Derbyshire

Dear Mr Ravenscroft

I am in receipt of your letter dated 19 March, for which I thank
you, but I think there has been some misunderstanding.

Firstly, I must re-iterate that our Inflight Meals are not available
for re-sale, and unfortunately we can not make any exceptions
to this policy.

With regard to our comment in the last paragraph of my letter,
I believe that you may have misinterpreted my meaning when
I stated that we would be pleased to welcome you on board
again in the near future. This of course referred to you choosing
to travel with us again and not an open invitation to a free
flight to sample our meals.

I apologise for any misunderstanding that this may have caused.

Yours sincerely

Peter Malden
Associate Director – Inflight Services

Company Registration No: 1966273 (England) Registered Office: Oakdale Broadfield Park Brighton Road Crawley West Sussex RH11 9RT

The Elms
Wenter Road
New Mills
High Peak
Derbyshire

The Chairman
Air 2000 Ltd
Oakdale Broadfield Park
Crawley
West Sussex
RH11 9RT

12th April

Dear Mr Chairman

On the 4th of March I wrote to Air 2000 saying that I had recently travelled with your airline and how much I had enjoyed the experience, particularly the lasagne coming back. On the 15th of March a Mr Peter Malden, Associate Director, Inflight Services, replied to my letter and invited me to have a free flight on one of your aeroplanes so I might sample your lasagne again. I thanked him for the letter, indicated to him when I would like to take up his kind offer, arranged to take some time off work, and told many of my friends about Air 2000's generous gesture. Then, in a letter sent to me which I received on April the 12th, a mere two days before I was due to fly, Mr Malden withdrew the invitation, saying that I had misinterpreted his letter and that he hadn't invited me at all! This quite frankly beggars belief! His exact words in his letter of the 15th March were '.....we would be very pleased to welcome you on board again in the near future to sample the refreshments within our service again.' Now if that isn't an invitation I don't know what is!

I am now in the embarrassing position of having a week off work with nothing to do, and your airline is the direct cause of my embarrassment. I would like to know what you intend to do about the situation you have placed me in, because if I don't get some satisfaction on this you can rest assured that the many friends to whom I spoke about Air 2000's generosity will be informed about how you renege on your promises!

Yours sincerely

T Ravenscroft (Mr)

P.S. Can you please get the catering firm who supply your in-flight meals to send me the recipe for their lasagne? Thank you.

AIR 2000

Air 2000 Limited Oakdale Broadfield Park Brighton Road Crawley West Sussex RH11 9RT Telephone : 0293 518966
Telex: 878434 Answerback AIRTWO G Facsimile: 0293 522927

26 April

Mr T Ravenscroft
The Elms
Wenter Road
New Mills
High Peak
Derbyshire

Dear Mr Ravenscroft

Thank you for your letter dated 12th April and, after reading all the correspondence involved between you and Air 2000 Limited, I can see that there has been some misinterpretation of the words in Mr Malden's letter to you dated 15th March.

We are very sorry that you feel that you have been misled, however I find it extraordinary that you could think that any airline would offer a passenger a free flight simply to sample the on-board refreshments.

Once again, please accept our apologies for any misunderstanding and for any inconvenience caused.

Yours sincerely

Ken Smith
Managing Director

Company Registration No: 1966273 (England) Registered Office: Oakdale Broadfield Park Brighton Road Crawley West Sussex RH11 9RT

Ken Smith
Managing Director
Air 2000 Ltd
Oakfield Broadfield Park
Brighton Road
CRAWLEY
West Sussex
RH11 9RT

5th May

Dear Mr Smith

Reference your letter dated April 26th.

I find it extraordinary that you find it extraordinary that any airline would offer a passenger a free flight simply to sample their on-board refreshments. But then I am a generous man, and, as it has now transpired, Air 2000 is perhaps not such a generous airline. Despite giving me a Mint Imperial both ways.

But to your lasagne. I am afraid I have some rather bad news for you. There is a good chance that it might not be as popular with your passengers as I may have led you to believe. Since opening my correspondence with Air 2000 three friends of mine to whom I recommended your airline have flown with you. Quite astonishingly, none of them liked your lasagne! (Although one of them said it might not have been lasagne, it might have been shepherd's pie, he wasn't sure. Anyway whatever it was he didn't like it). In fact my osteopath Mr Davies was quite uncomplimentary about your lasagne and told me that the next time I felt like recommending anything to him not to bother thank you very much; and what's more I am convinced he made me suffer much more than he usually does when he was manipulating my spine back into position, but perhaps that's just my imagination.

So it is a case of one man's meat being another man's poison I suppose. Quite possibly the three people in question don't have the advantage of my educated palate, and maybe if, like me, they dined regularly at McDonald's and Kentucky Fried Chicken they would know what good food tasted like.

By the way you have still to send me the recipe for your lasagne. After disappointing me with regard to your generosity I think it is the very least you can do.

Yours sincerely

T Ravenscroft (Mr)

The Elms
Wenter Road
New Mills
High Peak
Derbyshire

Britannia Airways Ltd
Britannia House   4th March
London Luton Airport Beds
LU2 9ND

Dear Britannia Airways

After years of wishing to fly away to some foreign clime for a
holiday but not being able to afford it, I am now in the position
to take a modest package holiday this summer. However before
I can do this there is a slight problem which must be addressed.
I weigh forty-two stone. And whilst realising that generously
proportioned men such as myself do manage to fly to holiday
destinations I also realise that there must be some upper limit
regarding passenger dimensions.

Having said that, I do know for a fact that your particular airline
flew a generously built acquaintance of mine to Spain last year,
although it must be admitted that at only twenty-six stone he is
somewhat lighter than me. This acquaintance told me that as it
was clear that his stomach would foul the back of the seat in
front of him, thus making it impossible for him to sit with any
degree of comfort, that you kindly arranged for him to have a
seat where there was nothing in front of him, near the door. This
arrangement worked admirably, and would probably work for
me too if it wasn't for the fact that with the best will in the world
I would never be able to squash myself into one of the narrow
seats that seem to be universally favoured by aeroplanes.

However I do know for a fact that it is possible to fly men as large
as me, because a couple of years ago a party of sumo wrestlers
from Japan flew into this country, and, as I'm sure you are aware,

sumo wrestlers don't exactly hold back with the chopsticks when it comes to eating. But perhaps they had special aeroplanes?

Is there anything that you can do for me, short of my having to pay for two seats near the door and having the chair arm removed from between them? I have considered travelling in the hold with the luggage but I don't really want to do this unless there is absolutely no alternative as I suffer from claustrophobia.

Yours faithfully

T Ravenscroft (Mr)

CHARTER AIRLINE OF THE YEAR

Our Ref : PAX/GEN/SS

8 April

Mr T Ravenscroft
The Elms
Wenter Road
New Mills
High Peak
Derbyshire

Dear Mr Ravenscroft

I refer to your letter dated 4th March and our subsequent telephone conversation.

Having discussed this matter further with our Inflight Safety Department, we do feel we may have some difficulty in accommodating you in one of our airline seats. However, we would like to invite you along to our training centre at East Midlands, where we have mockups of the aircraft. You would then be able to try the seats out for yourself, which would give us all a better insight as to how we could help you.

If you would like to take this opportunity please let me know quite soon and I can then make the necessary arrangements.

Yours sincerely

Sue Smith
Passenger Relations Officer

Britannia Airways Ltd. Britannia House. London Luton Airport. Bedfordshire. England. LU2 9ND
Telephone (0582) 424155   Facsimile (0582) 458594   Telex 82239
Head Office and Registered Office: London Luton Airport. Bedfordshire, England. Registered in England No. 444359

The Elms
Wenter Road
New Mills
High Peak
Derbyshire

Sue Smith
Passenger Relations Officer   22nd April
Britannia Airways Ltd
Britannia House
London Luton Airport Beds
LU2 9ND

Dear Sue Smith

Thank you for your letter of April 8th and the invitation to visit your training centre at East Midlands.

First of all I would like to clear up a little mistake, because inadvertently I wrote in my initial letter that I was forty-two stone. This was a mistake. I am actually only thirty-two stone. I bet you thought that I was a big fatty, didn't you!

In point of fact, and because I want to give myself the best chance possible of flying with Britannia this summer, I have for the last month been on a strict diet, with the result that I am now down to thirty-one stone ten-and-a-half pounds, and the weight is still simply dropping off me!

I accept your kind invitation, and would appreciate it if you could make the arrangements as soon as possible. I am free to visit you any day, but would prefer not to come on Wednesday as that is the night I go to Weightwatchers, or Thursday evening when I go to the pub.

Yours sincerely

T Ravenscroft (Mr)

Sue Smith
Passenger Relations Officer   18th May
Britannia Airways Ltd
Britannia House
London Luton Airport Beds
LU2 9ND

Dear Sue Smith

I had hoped that I would have heard from you by this time with news of when I might attend your East Midlands training centre to see if I can fit in one of your aeroplanes. I suppose that with so many thin people eager to take to the skies Britannia feel that they need not hurry themselves unduly in the matter of getting a fat one up there as well.

In point of fact I am fast becoming a thin person myself, thanks to dieting religiously since I last wrote to you. I am now down to a mere thirty-one stone six pounds! This means that I have now lost a total of eight pounds in only six weeks, which equates to roughly three stone, or eighty-four packets of butter a year.

Even the comparatively small amount of weight I have lost thus far has brought about a distinct improvement in my social life, as I am now able to get through the doors of the local Pussy Cat Nightclub. I visited this popular nighterie for the very first time last week and had a really enjoyable time – in fact too enjoyable because after I'd had a few drinks my resolve weakened and I rounded off the evening by gorging myself on the club special two-pounder T-bone steak and double french fries, with the result that I got wedged in the doorway on the way out and had to be pulled out by the bouncers.

I have worked out that if I continue to lose weight at the present rate I will be down to twelve stone in four years' time, or, to continue with the butter analogy, if I am a butter mountain now then two thirds of me will have been sold off cheaply to the Russians. Consequently I would no longer have the problem participating in air travel which I have at the moment. However four years is longer than I wish to wait so I would be most grateful if you could expedite my visit to your training centre without further delay.

Yours sincerely

T Ravenscroft (Mr)

Our Ref : PAX/GEN/SS

25 May

Mr T Ravenscroft
The Elms
Wenter Road
New Mills
High Peak
Derbyshire

Dear Mr Ravenscroft

Many thanks for your recent correspondence, but may I first apologise for the delay in responding.

Unfortunately due to a heavy workload replies have taken slightly longer than usual. I am pleased to inform you that we can actually arrange a visit to Manchester airport for you, which I believe would be a lot closer for you to travel to. If you could let me know which Monday afternoon suits you best I can then finalise the arrangements.

However, before the visit can take place, for security reasons, I will need to know your full name, full address, city of birth and date of birth. Then on the day of the visit you must take with you some form of identification, perhaps a driving licence or other official documentation.

I look forward to hearing from you very soon – you're doing really well – keep it up.

Yours sincerely

Sue Smith
Passenger Relations Officer

Britannia Airways Ltd. Britannia House. London Luton Airport. Bedfordshire. England. LU2 9ND
Telephone (0582) 424155   Facsimile (0582) 458594   Telex 82239
Head Office and Registered Office: London Luton Airport, Bedfordshire, England, Registered in England No. 444359

The Elms
Wenter Road
New Mills
High Peak
Derbyshire

Sue Smith
Passenger Relations Officer   26th May
Britannia Airways Ltd
Britannia House
London Luton Airport Beds
LU2 9ND

Dear Sue Smith

Thank you for your letter of May 25th. What good news! I can make myself available any Monday, and the sooner the better.

It is a pity that you need to have my full name since this is a constant source of embarrassment to me. However as it is the name on my birth certificate and this is the document I will be presenting to you as identification I have no alternative but to give it to you. My full name is – don't laugh – Terence Slim Ravenscroft. Apparently my mother was an avid fan of the Country and Western singer Slim Whitman, who I believe was very popular at the time of my birth, in the mid-fifties.

My address is as above, my place of birth is Stockport, and I was born in 1954 on the 9th of March.

Yours sincerely

T Ravenscroft (Mr)

P.S. Since last writing to you I have shed another two pounds. There will be nothing left of me at this rate!

CHARTER AIRLINE OF THE YEAR

Our Ref : PAX/GEN/SS

22 June

Mr T Ravenscroft
The Elms
Wenter Road
New Mills
High Peak
Derbyshire

Dear Mr Ravenscroft

Good News! – it's all systems go for next Monday.

If you could make arrangements to arrive at Manchester airport, terminal two, on Monday afternoon, the 27th June, for about 1.30 that would be great. You need to make your way to the airport information desk where there are some courtesy telephones. If you use the phone and dial ▮▮▮ that will get you through to our office and one of the staff on duty, possibly Julie, will come to meet you. You will then be escorted to the security unit to be issued with your ID card, so you must ensure that you carry your birth certificate with you.

I hope everything goes well and you enjoy your visit. Please do let me know how you get on.

Yours sincerely

Sue Smith
Passenger Relations Officer

Britannia Airways Ltd. Britannia House. London Luton Airport. Bedfordshire. England. LU2 9ND
Telephone (0582) 424155   Facsimile (0582) 458594   Telex 82239
Head Office and Registered Office: London Luton Airport, Bedfordshire, England. Registered in England No. 444359

The Elms
Wenter Road
New Mills
High Peak
Derbyshire

Sue Smith
Passenger Relations Officer   30th June
Britannia Airways Ltd
Britannia House
London Luton Airport Beds
LU2 9ND

Dear Sue Smith

Thank you for your letter dated 22nd June, which I did not receive until the evening of 27th June, too late for me to keep the appointment. Britannia Airways are evidently more efficient than Royal Mail!

Thank you for all your efforts to get me airborne but I am afraid that due to the incident described in full below I no longer wish to fly.

On Saturday my friend Charles called to pick me up as usual for our weekly visit to the greyhound racing at nearby Manchester. I am sure you will realise that a person of my dimensions can't get into a car but Charles has a pick-up truck that I sit in the back of, covered by a tarpaulin so that people won't laugh at me.

Soon after we set off Charles stopped to buy a packet of cigarettes, and whilst he was in the shop a thief stole the pick-up truck. I didn't know this at the time of course as I was under the tarpaulin, but I became suspicious when after we had been travelling for over an hour we still hadn't reached the greyhound stadium. I peeped out from under the tarpaulin to discover that we were on the M6 motorway! Through the glass panel at the back of the cab of the pick-up I could see that the driver was not Charles but the thief. At that very moment the thief saw me through the rear-view mirror, and was so surprised at the sight of a thirty-one-stone-plus hulk emerging from under the tarpaulin that he lost control of the truck, causing it to swerve violently. This was observed by a roadside police car, which quickly gave chase, sounding its siren and flashing its lights. However, far from pulling up the thief started to drive faster.

The next twenty minutes were an absolute nightmare, for the truck left the motorway at the next exit and the police car pursued it at speeds of up to a hundred miles an hour, with yours truly hanging on for dear life. Worse was to follow, because on rounding a bend on two wheels we were faced with a tractor pulling a load of hay, which had suddenly appeared out of a side road, and the thief had to stand on the brakes. The truck stopped immediately but unfortunately I didn't, and the impetus threw me out of the back of the truck, whereupon I sailed through the air some sixty yards before fortunately landing on the tractor's load of hay.

The incident left me severely traumatised, and on eventually getting back to Stockport I went to the doctor and requested a sedative. While I was with the doctor he remarked that when I was catapulted through the air from the truck and sailed through the air that it must have been just like flying. Well if that is like flying you can keep it!

Yours sincerely

T Ravenscroft (Mr)

END OF CORRESPONDENCE

The Elms
Wenter Road
New Mills
High Peak
Derbyshire

Airtours Airlines
Wavell House   15th March
Holcombe Road
Helmshore
Rossendale
Lancs
BB4 4NB

Dear Airtours Airlines

I recently travelled on one of your aeroplanes – I think it was a Boeing 767 – anyway it was the one with an enormous engine suspended precariously from each wing – and following the experience I have a rather serious complaint to make.

From where I was seated in seat 15A a good quarter of the TV screen was obscured from my view by the overhead hand-baggage compartment. The in-flight movie was 'Sister Act Two'. I saw about 'Sister Act One And A Half'. As it turned out this proved to be a blessing in disguise as the film was absolute bilge and the less one could see of it the better, but that is hardly the point.

Your TV screen being partially obscured from view is not my complaint however, although this situation is far from satisfactory. My complaint is that through leaning over in an effort to see all the TV screen (impossible), I got a stiff neck. When we arrived at our hotel I applied some 'Fiery Jack' to my neck to ease the pain. (Fortunately my wife always carries this ointment with her, it does wonders for her lumbago and I can thoroughly recommend it.)

However, before I had the chance to wash my hands after administering the Fiery Jack I was distracted by one of my children being sick. After dealing with this emergency I went to the toilet to urinate, forgetting that I still had traces of Fiery Jack on my hands, with the result that I severely burned my penis, which completely spoiled my holiday.

I have now thankfully recovered, but the fact remains that if you had taken the trouble to position the TVs in your Boeing 767s so that people sitting in seat 15A could see all the screen without getting a stiff neck then this would never have happened. Bearing this in mind I think that compensation for inconvenience and pain and suffering would be in order, and I await your reply with interest.

Yours sincerely

T Ravenscroft (Mr)

Our ref: SLB/NMB/Gen.

Mr T Ravenscroft
The Elms
Wenter Road
New Mills
High Peak
Derbyshire

Dear Mr Ravenscroft

RE; Flight.

Thank you for your letter relating to your holiday.

May I say how sorry I was to learn of your disappointment with your flight. Unfortunately, the layout and design of an aircraft is determined by the manufacturer and regrettably, the placement of T.V. screens, for example, rests with them and not the tour operator.

I am sorry that your holiday was not wholly enjoyed and I do hope Airtours will have the pleasure of arranging a further holiday for you sometime in the future.

Yours sincerely

SUE BARKER (MRS)
CUSTOMER SERVICES EXECUTIVE.

AIRTOURS PLC

Wavell House, Holcombe Road, Helmshore, Rossendale, Lancashire BB4 4NB

Tel 0706 830130 Telex 635126 Fax 0706 212144

Registered Office: Wavell House, Holcombe Road, Helmshore, Rossendale, Lancashire. ABTA Number 47064 ATOL Number 1179. Registered in England Number 742748

The Elms
Wenter Road
New Mills
High Peak
Derbyshire

Sue Barker
Airtours Airlines
Wavell House
Holcombe Road
Helmshore
Rossendale
Lancs BB4 4NB

10th April

Dear Airtours Airlines

Reference your letter of 20th March.

I am very disappointed with your reply to say the least. I certainly expected a much more responsible attitude from a British airline.

You would do well to take a leaf out of Marks and Spencer's book when it comes to customer service. This fine company refunded my wife's money without question when the 36D bra she had purchased from them turned out to be a 36B bra with a 36D label in it, with the result that she sustained pinched breasts.

To try to claim that the placement of your TV screens rests with the manufacturers of the aeroplane is quite simply passing the buck. It is your aeroplane and you can have it fitted out exactly as you see fit. The fact is that you are as guilty of purveying faulty goods just as surely as were MFI when they sold me a coffee table and the following day one of the legs fell off. I also notice that you conveniently avoided the issue of compensation.

As it seems that you are unwilling to face up to your obligations in this matter you leave me no alternative but to pursue the matter direct with Boeing.

Yours faithfully

T Ravenscroft (Mr)

The Elms
Wenter Road
New Mills
High Peak
Derbyshire

Mr M Hamilton
Boeing Commercial Airline Group   10th April
Room P3
Third Floor
Tech Block A
Heathrow Airport
Hounslow
Middlesex
TW6 2BH

Dear Mr Hamilton

I enclose a copy of a letter of complaint which I recently sent
to Airtours Airlines, and a copy of their reply. It would appear
that rightly or wrongly – although I must say it seems to me
they are passing the buck – they are placing the blame for the
incident squarely on the shoulders of Boeing. I would
appreciate your comments before I place this sorry matter in
the hands of my solicitors.

Have a nice day.

Yours sincerely

T Ravenscroft (Mr)

18th April

Mr T Ravenscroft
The Elms
Wenter Road
New Mills
High Peak
Derbyshire

Dear Mr Ravenscroft

RE; Flight.

Thank you for your further letter relating to your holiday.

Having carefully considered all that has been said, I find there is nothing further I can add to my initial response save apologise once more for any disappointment experienced.

If you wish for further investigations to be made, could you please provide your booking reference, your destination and your date of departure.

Yours sincerely

SUE BARKER (MRS)
CUSTOMER SERVICES EXECUTIVE.

AIRTOURS PLC

Wavell House, Holcombe Road, Helmshore, Rossendale, Lancashire BB4 4NB

Tel 0706 830130 Telex 635126 Fax 0706 212144

Registered Office: Wavell House, Holcombe Road, Helmshore, Rossendale, Lancashire. ABTA Number 47064 ATOL Number 1179. Registered in England Number 742748

Sue Barker
Customer Services Executive
Airtours Airlines
Wavell House
Holcombe Road
Hemshore
Rossendale
Lancs
BB4 4HB

The Elms
Wenter Road
New Mills
High Peak
Derbyshire

24th April

Dear Mrs Barker

Reference your letter of 18th April.

I am now corresponding direct with Boeing regarding this matter so any details from me about my flight would be irrelevant. I should imagine that the next communication you receive on the subject will either be from Boeing's solicitors or mine.

I am however in your debt, because through your attitude you have demonstrated to me just how easy it is to ride roughshod over people. I have in fact already put this lesson to good effect in my dry-cleaning business, when a lady customer complained that culottes I had dry-cleaned for her had shrunk, rendering them four inches short in the leg and uncomfortably tight in the groin. I informed her that this wasn't my fault but the fault of the people who had manufactured my dry-cleaning machine, and she went on her way quite happily, albeit limping slightly. You airline people may be short on morals but you are certainly long on knowing how to fob off your customers, and I thank you once again for this very useful tip.

Yours sincerely

T Ravenscroft (Mr)

Copy to:- The Chairman, Airtours Airlines PLC

Boeing International Corporation
First Floor, Cardinal Point
Newall Road
Heathrow Airport (London)
Hounslow, Middlesex TW6 2BH

Telephone 081 759 3301
Telex 8956971 BOEING G.
Fax 081 759 9784

April 26

DDT/94104L
Page 1 of 1

Mr T Ravenscroft
The Elms
Wenter Road
New Mills
High Peak
Derbyshire

BOEING

Dear Mr Ravenscroft,

Reference your letter of 18th April.

We write to acknowledge receipt of your letter (undated) addressed to Mr. M. Hamilton of our Customer Services division which has been passed to this office for response.

Unfortunately, the director who handles the Airtours account is currently on an overseas business trip, returning in two weeks time, however, upon his return he will be more than happy to discuss the contents of your letter (and its enclosures) with you. Prior to his return, please provide the undersigned with a daytime telephone number to enable him to speak to you personally.

Yours faithfully,

Daniella D.M. Turner (Mrs)
Office Manager

Incorporated with Limited Liability
in the State of Delaware

The Elms
Wenter Road
New Mills
High Peak
Derbyshire

Daniella D M Turner
Boeing International Corp   30th April
First Floor
Cardinal Point
Newall Road
Heathrow Airport
Hounslow
TW6 2BH

Dear Mrs Turner

Thank you for your letter of 26th April.

There would not be any point in my giving you my telephone
number because unfortunately I am partially deaf and totally
dumb, therefore any communications I have with the director
who handles the Airtours account will have to be of a written
nature. I look forward to hearing from your director when he
has returned from his business trip.

Yours sincerely

T Ravenscroft (Mr)

The Elms
Wenter Road
New Mills
High Peak
Derbyshire

Daniella D M Turner
Boeing International Corp   19th May
First Floor
Cardinal Point
Newall Road
Heathrow Airport
Hounslow
TW6 2BH

Dear Mrs Turner

I would refer you to your letter ref DDT/94/104L dated 26th
April.

I am still waiting to hear from your director on this matter.
Perhaps you could jog his memory?

It has occurred to me that many airlines now no longer use
stewardesses to demonstrate emergency equipment and
procedures, preferring to fulfil this obligation via TV screens.
I would therefore respectfully point out that all passengers
occupying window seats cannot see a significant proportion
of the demonstration, as they cannot see the screen, and will
thus be ill-equipped to carry out the correct procedure should
an emergency arise. This is obviously a far from satisfactory
state of affairs and I would be interested to have Boeing's
observations on this point before I take it up with the civil
aviation authorities. Have a nice day.

Yours sincerely

T Ravenscroft (Mr)

Boeing International Corporation
First Floor, Cardinal Point
Newall Road
Heathrow Airport (London)
Hounslow, Middlesex TW6 2BH

Telephone 081 759 3301
Telex 8956971 BOEING G.
Fax 081 759 9784

May 25

DMG/DDT/94/056L
Page 1 0f 1

Mr T Ravenscroft
The Elms
Wenter Road
New Mills
High Peak
Derbyshire

BOEING

Dear Mr Ravenscroft,

Thank you for your letter of 19th May.

May I first apoligize for the tardiness in responding to your previous correspondence, however, I have, for the past few months, been away on various overseas business trips.

I would welcome the opportunity of speaking with you personally; I too have a slight hearing disability and can sympathize with your concerns over telephone conversations, however, I firmly believe that a person to person call would be of far more value and benefit to you.

I look forward to hearing from you at your convenience.

Yours faithfully,

Douglas M Goseclose
Director

Douglas M Goseclose
Boeing International Corp
First Floor
Cardinal Point
Newall Road
Heathrow Airport
Hounslow
TW6 2BH

The Elms
Wenter Road
New Mills
High Peak
Derbyshire

26th May

Dear Mr Goseclose

Thank you for your letter of 25th May.

I sincerely hope that your various overseas business trips didn't include flights on Boeing aeroplanes where you were given a window seat and therefore couldn't see the in-flight movie and emergency procedures properly.

Your Daniella D M Turner obviously didn't tell you the full extent of my communications difficulties. Or perhaps you didn't hear her properly, being a bit deaf yourself? The fact is that as well as being partially deaf I am totally dumb. Compared to me Harpo Marx is loquacious. A person to person call is not therefore on, as while talking to someone who can't reply might be of benefit to you it most certainly would not be of benefit to me.

I implore you to write to me as soon as possible as to your intentions in dealing with this matter as I am fast running out of patience.

Yours sincerely

T Ravenscroft (Mr)

The Elms
Wenter Road
New Mills
High Peak
Derbyshire

Air UK Ltd
Stansted House   19th March
Stansted Airport
Essex
CM24 1QT

Dear Air UK

I recently travelled with your airline, and what an exciting
experience it was! It was the very first time that I have ever
flown, but you can rest assured I will be flying with Air UK on
many more occasions in the future if my first experience was
anything to go by. Everything about the flight was excellent –
although I have heard that Air 2000 could give you a run for
your money as far as the in-flight catering goes – but what
excited me the most was the sight of your stewardesses. How
lovely they looked in their smart Air UK uniforms! And this
gets me to the point of my letter. Is it possible to buy an Air UK
stewardess uniform? I'm sure that if my wife owned one and
she wore it at the appropriate time it would be all that was
needed to put a bit of spice back into our sex life.

I look forward eagerly to your reply.

Yours sincerely

T Ravenscroft (Mr)

Our Ref: LH/JT

23rd March

Mr T Ravenscroft
The Elms
Wenter Road
New Mills
High Peak
Derbyshire

Dear Mr Ravenscroft

Thank you very much for your letter of 19th March.

It was very kind of you to take the time and trouble to write and say how much you enjoyed your flight with us and we have noted your comments about our catering.

I am afraid that, for security reasons, no part of our uniform can be sold to a member of the public so we cannot help with your request.

I do hope you fly with us again in the future and thank you once again for your kind remarks.

Yours sincerely

J THOMPSON
Cabin Services Administrator

AIR UK LIMITED, STANSTED HOUSE, STANSTED AIRPORT, STANSTED, ESSEX CM 24 1QT. TEL:(0279)680146 TELEX:817312 FAX:(0279)680012

REGISTERED IN ENGLAND 398309 REGISTERED OFFICE: STANSTED HOUSE, STANSTED AIRPORT, STANSTED, ESSEX CM 24 1QT

J Thompson
Air UK Ltd
Stansted House
Stansted Airport
Essex
CM24 1QT

The Elms
Wenter Road
New Mills
High Peak
Derbyshire

26th March

Dear J Thompson

Thank you for your prompt reply to my letter of 19th March.

I was very sorry to learn that you are unable to sell me one of your stewardess uniforms. I am very keen to get my hands on one of them, and so is my wife, so perhaps you could let me have one which is about to be discarded? I am sure that there would be lots of wear left in your stewardesses' uniforms after they have been issued with new ones, since I have yet to see a stewardess in anything other than a quite immaculate uniform. My wife is a wide-hipped size 12, so a size 14 or a size 12 which has been worn and stretched a little by one of your stewardesses who should really be wearing a size 14 would be lovely.

You need have no worries whatsoever about security because you have my word as a gentleman that the uniform will never leave our bedroom.

Regarding the catering. I don't think that it would be amiss of me to tell you that the jewel in Air 2000's crown is a quite breathtaking lasagne, so the next time I travel with Air UK perhaps I will see it on the menu? Served by one of your lovely stewardesses. Heaven!

Yours sincerely

T Ravenscroft (Mr)

Our Ref: JT/AN

12th April

Mr T Ravenscroft
The Elms
Wenter Road
New Mills
High Peak
Derbyshire

Dear Mr Ravenscroft

Thank you for your letter of 26th March.

I am afraid that we cannot accommodate your request. All second hand uniform which is still wearable is re-issued and anything else which is not serviceable is destroyed.

Yours sincerely

JENNIE THOMPSON
<u>Cabin Services Administrator</u>

AIR UK LIMITED, STANSTED HOUSE, STANSTED AIRPORT, STANSTED, ESSEX CM 24 1QT. TEL:(0279)680146 TELEX: 817312 FAX:(0279)680012

REGISTERED IN ENGLAND 398309 REGISTERED OFFICE: STANSTED HOUSE, STANSTED AIRPORT, STANSTED, ESSEX CM 24 1QT

The Elms
Wenter Road
New Mills
High Peak
Derbyshire

Jennie Thompson
Cabin Services Administrator   17th April
Air UK Ltd
Stansted House
Stansted Airport
Essex
CM24 1QT

Dear Jennie Thompson

Reference your letter of 12th April.

I am really disappointed with you. I would have expected someone with a pretty name like Jennie to be more understanding. You had the chance to make a man very happy and for reasons best known to yourself have seen fit to turn it down. Not only that, you then torture me by telling me that you actually destroy perfectly good stewardesses' uniforms, when just one of them might completely rejuvenate my sex life! What a spoilsport you are, Jennie. I will never travel with Air UK again!

Yours tearfully

T Ravenscroft (Mr)

PS. How about just a stewardesses' hat then?

44

Cyprus Airways
Euston Centre   31st March
29/31 Hampstead Road
LONDON
NW1 3JA

Dear Cyprus Airways

I would love to visit Cyprus for a holiday, but unfortunately there is one thing stopping me, for despite my being as British as John Bull himself I look extremely Turkish. I have a swarthy complexion, a dusky olive skin, jet black hair and limpid brown eyes. I also have a thick, droopy moustache which has the effect of making me look even more Turkish than I already look. I could of course shave off my moustache, but unfortunately I have a rather unsightly harelip, and on balance I would rather look Turkish than stupid.

I gather that relations between the Greeks and the Turks are somewhat dodgy to say the least, and quite naturally the last thing that I want whilst on holiday is to be hounded and unfairly treated by the indigenous population. There is no doubt whatsoever that I would be mistaken for a Turk as last year my wife and I and three other couples went to Turkey for our holidays, and it was quite noticeable that I was the only one of our party not to be constantly pestered by carpet salesmen. In fact one day when I was browsing in the bazaar a Turkish salesman asked me to mind his stall for a few minutes while he went for a haircut, and I almost sold a carpet to two Germans.

However, and despite the handicap of looking Turkish, I would still like to visit Aphrodite's Isle. Perhaps the situation isn't quite as bad as I have been led to believe, and the hostility felt by Greeks and Turks to each other has been exaggerated? My wife fancies the Paphos area, and if Turk-hating isn't too bad in Paphos I might just be persuaded to risk it. What do you think?

Yours faithfully

T Ravenscroft (Mr)

CYPRUS AIRWAYS

April 4

Mr T Ravenscroft
The Elms
Wenter Road
New Mills
High Peak
Derbyshire

Dear Mr Ravenscroft

Thank you for your letter of March 31 in regard to your proposed visit to Cyprus.

Having carefully considered your comments and studied various anthropological books - including Darwin's 'Theory of Evolution' - I would conclude that with the exception of your moustache, your appearance would conform to that of any male from countries bordering the Mediterranean. However, if you add the moustache and go to Cyprus, I feel certain that the population will think of you as a relative of Zorba, get you to dance the sirtaki while balancing a pyramid of glass containing 'zivanier' - Cyprus's white spirit - on your head. As this will be a case of Greek meeting Greek, or should I say the Paphian meeting Greek and since both will be conversing in English, I feel sure your holiday will be very enjoyable. And always remember the Cypriots philosophy of xenos - the stranger is welcome - which after all was Aphrodite's inheritance!

Yours sincerely

Geoffrey Matthews
Passenger Relations Adviser

CYPRUS AIRWAYS LIMITED
Euston Centre, 29/31 Hampstead Road, London NW1 3JA
Reservations 071 388 5411 (8 lines), Fares 071 3883225 (2 lines)
Sales 071 388 7981 (2 lines), Accounts 071 388 7547 (2 lines)
Administration 071 383 4831, Facsimile 071 3830126,
Telex 23881; Cables CYPRUSAIR London

The Elms
Wenter Road
New Mills
High Peak
Derbyshire

Geoffrey Matthews
Cyprus Airways
Euston Centre
29/31 Hampstead Road
LONDON
NW1 3JA

6th April

Dear Cyprus Airways

Thank you for your prompt reply to my letter of 31st March.

You seem to have gone to a lot of trouble on my behalf – and to good effect too, because you have laid to rest the fears I had about visiting Cyprus so completely that my wife and I intend to visit your lovely island in early May.

However, instead of spending the entire fortnight in Paphos, we are now leaning towards a two-centre holiday, the first week in Paphos and the second week somewhere in the north of the island, probably Kyrenia. Unfortunately I haven't seen this particular holiday in any of the brochures, so it appears that I will have to organise it myself. To this end, is it possible to fly by Cyprus Airways to Paphos and return from Kyrenia two weeks later? And if so, do Cyprus Airways operate an internal flight from Paphos to Kyrenia, or will we have to transfer there by some other method?

Thanking you for all that you have done for me thus far, and looking forward to your reply.

Yours faithfully

T Ravenscroft (Mr)

CYPRUS AIRWAYS

April 11

Mr T Ravenscroft
The Elms
Wenter Road
New Mills
High Peak
Derbyshire

Dear Mr Ravenscroft

Having received your letter of April 6, I am pleased to learn
of your intention to visit Paphos.

However, I am somewhat concerned by your ideas for a two
centre holiday as the Cyprus Government are not particularly
happy about tourists visiting Kyrenia. In fact, if you have a
Northern Cyprus entry stamp in your passport they will not
even allow you into the country.

Similarly, no Cyprus Airways flights fly to the north of the
Island nor can Tour Operators offer holidays which cover both
areas. The reason, as I am sure you are aware, being that
Turkey invaded Cyprus in 1974 and annexed a segment which
roughly covers an area just north of Ayia Napa, bisects
Nicosia and ends at Kato Pyrgos on the north east. (see
attached map)

I can therefore only suggest that if you want a two-centre
holiday you consider Paphos and another resort south of the
yellow line.

Yours sincerely

Geoffrey Matthews
Passenger Relations Adviser

CYPRUS AIRWAYS LIMITED
Euston Centre, 29/31 Hampstead Road, London NW1 3JA
Reservations 071 388 5411 (6 lines), Fares 071 3883225 (2 lines)
Sales 071 388 7981 (2 lines), Accounts 071 388 7547 (2 lines)
Administration 071 383 4831, Facsimile 071 3830126.
Telex 23881; Cables CYPRUSAIR London

The Elms
Wenter Road
New Mills
High Peak
Derbyshire

Geoffrey Matthews
Cyprus Airways
Euston Centre   15th April
29/31 Hampstead Road
LONDON
NW1 3JA

Dear Geoffrey Matthews

Thank you for your letter of 11th April. I had no idea that
booking a holiday on your island was going to be so complicated
– I certainly didn't have this trouble when we went to the Isle of
Wight!

I am afraid that you are wrong in your supposition that I knew
Turkey invaded Cyprus in 1974. I was in my late teens in 1974
and like all red-blooded male teenagers was heavily into girls.
A skirmish in the Mediterranean would have been the last
thing to attract my attention. Add to this the fact that TV
commercials for holidays in Cyprus always refer to it as 'The Isle
of Oranges and Sunshine' or 'The Isle of Aphrodite', and never
to my knowledge as 'The Isle that Turkey Invaded in 1974', and
it becomes quite understandable why someone living in a
country 2000 miles away might not have heard of your bit of
trouble. Perhaps if Britain had been involved in it in any way I
might have heard of it. However, it has now become clear to
me why the Greeks hold the Turks in such contempt and for
that I thank you.

Referring back to my original letter, and the matter of my
looking Turkish, might it not be better for me to have a two-
centre Cyprus holiday in the Turkish bit, say Kyrenia and
Famagusta? Or would you say from your experience that Greeks

and Turks look very much alike anyway – as I've been told – in which case a two-centre Paphos/Limassol holiday would be the one to plump for.

Either way a Cyprus holiday is now very definitely on the cards. I can't wait to dance the sirtaki whilst balancing a pyramid of glasses on my head! Seriously though, both my wife and I are looking forward very much to visiting Cyprus, no matter which half it is.

Yours faithfully

T Ravenscroft (Mr)

CYPRUS AIRWAYS

April 21

Mr T Ravenscroft
The Elms
Wenter Road
New Mills
High Peak
Derbyshire

Dear Mr Ravenscroft

Thank you for your letter of April 15 in regard to your holiday.

Having noted your comments about 1974, I appreciate that being
somewhat more ancient than you, possibly in between chasing
females, I did spend some time losing my home in Kyrenia!

However, though the TV commercials publicise Cyprus - at least
the area recognised as being Cyprus by most of the world's
Governments - as the Island of Aphrodite, a number of recent
documentaries on TV have covered the tragic events that
divided two communities who had lived in harmony for
a couple of centuries and only ended up as enemies because of
factors outside the people's control. Similarly, though
Britain is 2000 miles away, Cyprus before it became a Republic
was a British colony and still retains Sovereign Rights on
bases at Dhekelia (outside Larnaca) and Akrotiri (outside
Paphos). As both bases are on the main highway joining Paphos
and Ayia Napa, it would be wise to note that British and not
Cypriot laws are strictly enforced while driving through
(eg: speed limits, breathalysers and seat belts).

As far as having a two centre holiday in Kyrenia and
Famagusta is concerned, the former is possible but I hardly

CYPRUS AIRWAYS LIMITED
Euston Centre, 29/31 Hampstead Road, London NW1 3JA
Reservations 071 388 5411 (8 lines), Fares 071 3883225 (2 lines)
Sales 071 388 7981 (2 lines), Accounts 071 388 7547 (2 lines)
Administration 071 383 4831, Facsimile 071 3830126,
Telex 23881, Cables CYPRUSAIR London

think the latter - which is now a ghost town of once luxury hotels - would suit either your wife or yourself.

However, if you wish to go, you may find the attached Jules Verne brochure interesting, but personally - as Cyprus is only 180 miles from East to West would suggest staying in Larnaca and driving to the other resorts.

Yours sincerely

Geoffrey Matthews
Passenger Relations Adviser

Geoffrey Matthews
Cyprus Airways
Euston Centre
29/31 Hampstead Road
LONDON
NW1 3JA

The Elms
Wenter Road
New Mills
High Peak
Derbyshire

26th April

Dear Geoffrey Matthews

Thank you for the Jules Verne brochure and the lesson in military history. The next time it's my turn to set the questions for our pub quiz league I will certainly include a question on Cyprus – I bet not many people know that it was once a British colony!

My wife and I have finally decided on Ayia Napa for our holiday. I booked the holiday yesterday, from the 18th of May to the 1st of June, flying by Cyprus Airways of course. Despite your disapproval, whilst staying in Ayia Napa we intend to visit Northern Cyprus for a couple of days, provided I can hire a moto-cross motorbike. I have studied a large-scale map of Cyprus and there would appear to be lots of places where we'll be able to slip into the Turkish bit without troubling the Customs people.

Once we are there I don't think that there is much chance of my being asked for identification papers because, as I've already mentioned, I look Turkish, and will therefore blend in with the locals. My wife, being the English Rose type, will stand out a little, but from what I've heard it is by no means uncommon for a Turk to have a white wife or mistress, so I am not anticipating too many problems.

I'm sorry to hear you lost your house in Kyrenia, as I know what it's like to get behind with the mortgage myself, but happily I managed to get myself sorted out before I lost mine.

Yours faithfully

T Ravenscroft (Mr)

CYPRUS AIRWAYS

April 29

Mr T Ravenscroft
The Elms
Wenter Road
New Mills
High Peak
Derbyshire

Dear Mr Ravenscroft

Thank you for your letter of April 26 in regard to your
holiday in Ayia Napa.

However, having noted your intentions to visit North Cyprus
illegally, I would discourage such action on a number of
grounds. As I am sure you are aware, large scale maps of the
area can not only be out of date, but do not show the 'no go'
areas patrolled by the United Nations midway between the two
countries, nor the fact that any routes bisecting the 'line'
are covered by watch towers on both sides of the 'yellow' line.

Additionally, though you may not be asked for passports
while touring the north, these will certainly be asked for
should you check-in to an hotel or taverna. While the North
Cyprus Authorities may overlook the irregularities as to
your method of entry, they may stamp your passport showing
entry. If this happens, I can assure you that Immigration at
Larnaca Airport will prevent you returning to the UK as
booked, levy a fine and deport you at your own cost.

As Loyd Grossman says 'Now its over to you!'
Yours sincerely

Geoffrey Matthews
Passenger Relations Adviser

CYPRUS AIRWAYS LIMITED
Euston Centre, 29/31 Hampstead Road, London NW1 3JA
Reservations 071 388 5411 (8 lines), Fares 071 3883225 (2 lines)
Sales 071 388 7981 (2 lines), Accounts 071 388 7547 (2 lines)
Administration 071 383 4831, Facsimile 071 3830126.
Telex 23881: Cables CYPRUSAIR London

The Elms
Wenter Road
New Mills
High Peak
Derbyshire

Geoffrey Matthews
Cyprus Airways
Euston Centre
29/31 Hampstead Road
LONDON
NW1 3JA

3rd June

Dear Geoffrey Matthews

Just a few lines to let you know how much my wife and I enjoyed our holiday in Cyprus. Your island was all that I thought it would be, and more besides.

Happily your fears that I might get into trouble should I enter Northern Cyprus were unfounded, although I must admit that I took the precaution of getting my wife to wear long flowing robes and a yashmak. Crossing the border at midnight with her on the pillion of my hired motorbike I felt quite like Lawrence of Arabia! The only time I was asked for my passport during our three days in the Turkish bit was when booking into a small hotel in Kyrenia. However before handing over the passport for inspection I took the precaution of inserting a ten-pound note between its pages, and any suspicions that the hotelier may have harboured disappeared along with the tenner.

We both found Kyrenia to be absolutely beautiful. I suppose that one day you hope to return there and set up home again, that is if you are still able to get a mortgage in the Turkish bit after what happened last time.

Ayia Napa was most pleasant too, as were the Greek Cypriots. As you predicted they showed me no animosity whatsoever, despite my Turkish appearance, except that is for the goatherd who spat at me, but I think that was due to my running over one of his goats with my motorbike rather than my looking Turkish.

I will most certainly be visiting both bits of Cyprus again and will thoroughly recommend Aphrodite's Isle to all my friends.

Yours faithfully

T Ravenscroft (Mr)

Monarch Airlines Ltd
London Luton Airport
LUTON
Beds
LU2 9NU

The Elms
Wenter Road
New Mills
High Peak
Derbyshire

26th March

Dear Monarch Airlines

Returning from Malaga by Monarch Airlines recently I purchased drinks for my wife and myself from your trolley. The cost of the drinks came to £3.50 sterling, and I was informed by your stewardess – a very attractive uniform by the way, although not quite as exciting as the Air UK uniform – that I could if I wished pay in Spanish pesetas and receive my change in sterling. This I agreed to and gave her a 1000 peseta note, value £5 at the going exchange rate. Imagine my surprise then when I received not the £1.50 change I was expecting but £1.20. I queried this with your stewardess and she assured me that all was in order.

I did not pursue the matter further at this juncture as I have always found it a sound policy in life not to argue with the staff but to go directly to the top. I would expect you to make a small handling charge of course, say the one to two per cent charged by banks and bureaux de change, but to charge a rate of twenty per cent would be tantamount to piracy at high altitude, so I can only assume that your stewardess made a miscalculation. I certainly don't think for one moment that an airline of Monarch's eminence would stoop to such usury, and I therefore look forward to the return of my thirty pence, and remain,

Yours faithfully

T Ravenscroft (Mr)

Monarch Airlines

MONARCH AIRLINES LIMITED
LONDON LUTON AIRPORT LUTON BEDS. LU2 9NU
Telephone: 0582 400000   Facsimile: 0582 411000
Telex: 825624   Sita: LTNAPZB

Direct Telephone: ....
Direct Facsimile: ....
Direct Telex: ....

8th April

Mr T Ravenscroft
The Elms
Wenter Road
New Mills
High Peak
Derbyshire

Dear Mr Ravenscroft

Thank you for your recent correspondence. The Peseta rate onboard at the time you flew with us was 225 Pesetas to the Pound. We do in fact make a passenger announcement to say that this is the Monarch rate and not the current Bank Rate and this is also stated in our Inflight Price List under the payment section (copy enclosed). Therefore, the 1000 Peseta note you tendered had a U.K. value to Monarch of £4.44. If the goods had cost £3.50 you should have actually received change of 94 pence. It would appear that the Cabin Crew actually gave you 26 pence too much change.

I hope the above clarifies the situation and assure you of our best intentions at all times.

Yours sincerely

R.J. Lewis
Cabin Services Manager

REG. OFFICE: 86 Broomfield Road, Chelmsford, Essex CM1 1SW REG. No. 907593 ENGLAND

The Elms
Wenter Road
New Mills
High Peak
Derbyshire

R J Lewis
Cabin Services Manager
Monarch Airlines Ltd   17th April
London Luton Airport
LUTON
Beds
LU2 9NU

Dear Mr Lewis

Reference your correspondence dated 8th April.

I find the contents of this letter quite astonishing! The exchange rate in Malaga at the time in question meant that 200 pesetas could be exchanged for one pound, yet a poundsworth of goods bought on your aeroplane cost 225 pesetas, a twelve and a half per cent difference in your favour – and the banks in Malaga which were giving 200 pesetas to the pound were making a profit!

I would be interested to learn how you can justify charging such exorbitant rates merely to change money, and I am sure that the Office of Fair Trading would be interested as well.

You are most definitely in the wrong business. Take my advice and forget all about flying aeroplanes for a living and go into the merchant banking racket. With your financial expertise and brass neck you would make a fortune. Failing that I think you ought to seriously consider changing the name of your airline from Monarch Airlines to Shylock Airlines. This would at least give your passengers some idea of what might be in store for them should they make the mistake of purchasing something from you.

I enclose postage stamps to the value of 26 pence, this being the amount I would appear to owe you, having been given 'too much change'!

Yours sincerely

T Ravenscroft (Mr)

Monarch Airlines

MONARCH AIRLINES LIMITED
LONDON LUTON AIRPORT LUTON BEDS. LU2 9NU
Telephone: 0582 400000 Facsimile: 0582 411000
Telex: 825624 Sita: LTNAPZB

Direct Telephone: ....
Direct Facsimile: ....
Direct Telex: ....

Our ref: RJL/CH

21st April

Mr T Ravenscroft
The Elms
Wenter Road
New Mills
High Peak
Derbyshire

Dear Mr Ravenscroft

Thank you for your recent letter, your comments are noted and I confirm receipt of the stamps to the value of 26 pence.

Assuming you of our best intentions at all times.

Yours sincerely

R.J. Lewis
Cabin Services Manager

REG. OFFICE: 66 Broomfield Road, Chelmsford, Essex CM1 1SW REG. No. 907593 ENGLAND

The Elms
Wenter Road
New Mills
High Peak
Derbyshire

R J Lewis
Cabin Services Manager
Monarch Airlines Ltd
London Luton Airport
LUTON
Beds
LU2 9NU

25th April

Dear Mr Lewis

Reference your letter of 21st April.

Perhaps it's not such a good idea for Monarch Airlines to go into the merchant banking business after all. Your financial expertise may not be as impressive as I at first thought as you spent 25 pence of the 26 pence I sent you on a first-class stamp to acknowledge receipt of it. Still, as a company who charges twelve and a half per cent plus merely for changing money you probably feel that you can well afford it.

Yours sincerely

T Ravenscroft (Mr)

END OF CORRESPONDENCE

The Elms
Wenter Road
New Mills
High Peak
Derbyshire

British Midland
Donington Hall
Castle Donington
DERBY
DE74 2SB

17th April

Dear British Midland

I am writing this letter on behalf of a friend who hasn't got the gift of letter writing.

In a few weeks' time my friend and his wife will be travelling with your airline to Amsterdam (lucky devils!). My friend would like to know that in the event that his wife happens to be seated next to a window, and the window suddenly shattered, say from being accidentally struck by a sharp blow with a hard blunt object like a masonry hammer, would his wife be sucked out of the window and fall to her death?

My friend would also like to know if the person sitting next to his wife would be safe from also being sucked out along with his wife if he'd taken the precaution of fastening his seat belt first.

Thank you

Yours sincerely

T Ravenscroft (Mr)

British Midland
Donington Hall
Castle Donington
Derby DE74 2SB

Telephone Derby (0332) 854000
International +44 (332) 854000
Fax (0332) 854662
Telex 37172 BMAOBD G
Sita EMACOBD

British Midland

Mr T Ravenscroft
The Elms
Wenter Road
New Mills
High Peak
Derbyshire

29th April

Dear Mr Ravenscroft

Thank you for your letter dated 17th April,
concerning your friends journey to Amsterdam
with us, in the next few weeks.

I did try to telephone you to discuss the
issues raised in your letter but clearly you
are very busy at the moment.

For your information, the windows of the
aircraft are multilayered and therefore able to
withstand the impact of most items striking
against them. However, the item that you
mentioned by way of an example, a masonry
hammer, would not be permitted on the aircraft.
Each customer travelling on a flight has to
pass through security checks during which
anything deemed to be an offensive weapon is
confiscated. It is highly unlikely therefore
that anyone would be on-board an aircraft, with
an item capable of smashing an aircraft window.
Any accidental form of window breakage is
also extremely unlikely. In the event of a

British Midland Airways Limited Registered number: 464648 England   Registered office: Donington Hall Castle Donington Derby DE7 2SB

window breaking, it is unlikely that anyone would be sucked out, as it is common practice now for all airlines to request their customers to keep their seat belts fastened during the journey.

I know you will appreciate that aircraft today are built to offer maximum safety to customers on-board, and the scenario you have suggested to me, I feel, is unlikely with a commercial airline.

On behalf of British Midland may I thank you for taking the time and trouble to write to me with your concerns, and I hope that I have managed to answer these particular points to your satisfaction.

Yours sincerely

Ian Bloor
Customer Service Manager

The Elms
Wenter Road
New Mills
High Peak
Derbyshire

Ian Bloor
Customer Services Manager   5th May
British Midland
Donington Hall
Castle Donington
DERBY
DE74 2SB

Dear Mr Bloor

Thank you for your letter of 29th April.

I showed it to my friend and he has decided to go by boat instead.

Yours sincerely

T Ravenscroft (Mr)

END OF CORRESPONDENCE

The Elms
Wenter Road
New Mills
High Peak
Derbyshire

Lufthansa German Airlines   28th March
Lufthansa House
10 Old Bond Street
LONDON

Dear Lufthansa Airlines

I will be taking a party of wine-lovers to Germany this summer for an informal tour of the Mosel and Ruhr valleys. As I have always been most impressed with German engineering and efficiency – I did my National Service in Minden, Westphalia so I know what I am talking about, having seen it at first hand – and as I have also received very good reports on the Lufthansa in-flight catering I have decided to fly with your airline. If your bratwurst and pumpernickel are up to the standard of Air 2000's lasagne then we are in for a rare treat.

Rather than fly on one of your scheduled flights I would like to charter one of your aeroplanes, if that is at all possible. Not too large a one of course, as that wouldn't make economic sense. I don't exactly know what you have in your hangars at the moment, but an aeroplane about the size of the German one in the film 'The Heroes Of Telemark', which I have been reliably informed was a Heinkel Bomber, would be admirable – although that aeroplane in particular had machine-gun turrets front and back if my memory serves me correctly, and we wouldn't want it to have those of course.

Incidentally, if you haven't seen 'The Heroes Of Telemark' it is one of the best war films it has been my pleasure to see, and I can thoroughly recommend it. I am sure you would enjoy it too, even though your side doesn't win.

We wish to travel around the 25th of May and return, with lots of lovely German wines, three weeks later. I look forward to hearing from you with flying times and prices.

Yours sincerely

T Ravenscroft (Mr)

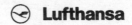

Lufthansa German Airlines
2nd Floor, Olympic House, Manchester Airport, Manchester M22 5QX

Your Ref.
Ihre Zeichen

Our Ref./Date
Unsere Zeichen/Datum

Telephone-Ext.
Telefon-Durchw.

Mr T Ravenscroft
The Elms
Wenter Road
New Mills
High Peak
Derbyshire

12 April

Dear Mr Ravenscroft

Thank you for your letter.

We too hope you will enjoy our onboard catering although
we can't guarantee bratwurst or pumpernickel!

You mentioned in your letter that you would like to
charter an aircraft. Because our smallest aircraft is a
50 seater and there would be two empty ferry legs we
think the cost per seat would be prohibitive, especially
in comparison to some of the special fares now on offer.
The cheapest at present would be the 'GSX or Seat Sale'
fares. These are £124.00 from Manchester to Dusseldorf
and £150.00 to Frankfurt. There is a German security tax
of £2.60 payable on each ticket. The fares are valid for
up to one month and have a minimum stay requirement of
a Saturday night, i.e. you must have a Saturday night in
your stay in Germany. Once the seats have been booked and
paid for no changes or refunds are allowed so we
recommend an insurance is taken out to guard against any
unforeseen events which might cause a change of plan.
You should book early as seats at these fares are limited

For corporate details, address and
further information p.t.o.
Gesellschaftsrechtliche Angaben,
Anschrift und weitere Informationen
auf der Rückseite

and our telephone number for reservations is ███████████.
We have also enclosed a copy of our current timetable.

Thank you once again for writing to us and we hope the above will be of help when planning the holiday. If you should require further information about bookings or fares don't hesitate to call us on that number.

Assuring you of our best attention at all times, we remain,

Yours sincerely

Alastair Raine
Reservations Supervisor
Lufthansa German Airlines
Northern England & Northern Ireland.

The Elms
Wenter Road
New Mills
High Peak
Derbyshire

Alastair Raine
Lufthansa German Airlines   16th April
Lufthansa House
10 Old Bond Street
LONDON

Dear Mr Raine

Thank you for your letter of 12th April and the copy of your current timetable and aircraft complement.

Despite what you wrote about the cost of chartering one of your smaller aeroplanes being prohibitive, I would still like to pursue the matter. This is because since writing to you another four wine-lovers have intimated that they would like to join our party, making a total of twenty-four wine-lovers in all. However, and more importantly, our ranks will be further swelled by the addition of twenty-two members of the New Mills and District Royal Air Force Veterans and Sons of Veterans Society, who will be visiting the Ruhr as part of their annual celebration of the bombing of the Moehne Dam. As you can imagine the prospect of flying in a fifty-seater Fokker is most appealing to them. This will make forty-six passengers in all and I am sure that I'll be able to get another four wine-lovers, or New Mills and District Royal Air Force Veterans and Sons of Veterans, before the 25th May or thereabouts.

I am assuming of course that chartering the little Fokker will work out cheaper than purchasing fifty tickets at £150 per ticket, which is remarkably cheap for a flight to Germany, if I may say so. (It cost me almost as much as that the last time I flew from Manchester to London, but that's your German efficiency shining through I suppose.)

However I am sure that you will point me towards whichever option is the most economical way of doing things, and I look forward to receiving your reply.

Yours sincerely

T Ravenscroft (Mr)

Lufthansa German Airlines
2nd Floor, Olympic House, Manchester Airport, Manchester M22 5QX

Your Ref.
Ihre Zeichen

Our Ref./Date
Unsere Zeichen/Datum

Telephone-Ext.
Telefon-Durchw.

Mr T Ravenscroft
The Elms
Wenter Road
New Mills
High Peak
Derbyshire

MANG513-R 6th May

Dear Mr Ravenscroft

Thank you for your letter of 16th April.

Please forgive the delay in replying but we have now received the charter offer from our sister company Lufthansa City Line who operate the 50 seater Fokker F.50s. Unfortunately it is as we suggested in our original reply, very expensive in comparison with the published fares. The cost would be £21,454.00 or £429.00 per person, which I'm sure you will agree is rather prohibitive.

We look forward to hearing from you with your decision and remain,

Yours sincerely
Lufthansa German Airlines

Alastair Raine
Reservations Supervisor
Northern England & Northern Ireland.

For corporate details, address and
further information p.t.o.
Gesellschaftsrechtliche Angaben,
Anschrift und weitere Informationen
auf der Rückseite

The Elms
Wenter Road
New Mills
High Peak
Derbyshire

Alastair Raine
Lufthansa German Airlines   12th May
Lufthansa House
10 Old Bond Street
LONDON

Dear Mr Raine

Thank you for your letter of 6th May.

You are right, the cost of hiring the Fokker is indeed prohibitive. Flying by scheduled as opposed to chartered aeroplane doesn't really make much difference to the wine-lovers and me. However the New Mills Royal Air Force Veterans and Sons of Veterans are very disappointed, as they were really looking forward to the experience – names like Fokker and Messerschmitt being far more evocative to their ears than Boeing and Airbus.

They also feel that had we chartered the Fokker we would have had more control over your intended flight path, and that those ex-RAF men wishing to parachute into Germany would have been able to come down in your country more or less exactly where they wanted to, whereas if we travel on one of your scheduled flights they may have to parachute out of your door some distance from where they actually wish to land.

I have now instructed our travel agent to book the seats with Lufthansa and I thank you for all your help.

Yours sincerely

T Ravenscroft (Mr)   **END OF CORRESPONDENCE**

The Elms
Wenter Road
New Mills
High Peak
Derbyshire

British Airways
Heathrow Airport   26th March
Hounslow
Middlesex

Dear British Airways

I feel I must write to you about an incident which occurred
when I recently 'flew the flag' with BA. At the check-in desk
your girl informed a passenger that his baggage was almost a
kilogram overweight. Being a couple of places in the queue
behind the passenger I wasn't close enough to catch the
entire conversation – probably a charge for excess baggage
was mooted – but the upshot was that the passenger then
opened his suitcase, produced two half-kilogram blocks of
chocolate, and proceeded to eat them, thus rendering his
baggage acceptable.

As chance would have it I was seated next to the passenger in
question on the aeroplane. All went without incident until
about halfway through the flight when the passenger was
suddenly violently sick, splattering my suede Hush Puppies
and completely ruining them. The reason for his illness is not
certain – possibly the meal that we had been served half an
hour previously had something to do with it as I noticed that
several people left it – though personally I found it quite
acceptable, though I didn't eat the pink thing which smelled
of fish. (It must be said however that your catering is way
below the standard reached by Air 2000. You would do well
to try to get their recipe for lasagne.) However, I prefer to
think that the cause of the passenger's biliousness was the
vast amount of chocolate he had consumed prior to getting
on the aeroplane.

The above incident raises three points:-

(a) Your check-in girl causing the passenger to eat the chocolate was futile to say the least, since the total weight of the passenger and his baggage was precisely the same both before and after he had eaten the chocolate.

(b) The passenger only weighed about nine stone. I myself weigh close to eighteen stone and I am quite sure that my weight added to my baggage was greater than the passenger's weight added to his baggage, so your system is clearly unfair.

(c) If either (a) or (b) had been taken into consideration, and any degree of common sense had been applied, the passenger would have been allowed onto the aeroplane without being coerced into eating the chocolate, and he would not have thrown up on my Hush Puppies.

I would appreciate your comments on the above before I take further action.

Yours faithfully

T Ravenscroft (Mr)

19th April

Mr T Ravenscroft
The Elms
Wenter Road
New Mills
High Peak
Derbyshire

British Airways Plc
PO Box 10 (S506)
Heathrow Airport
Hounslow
Middlesex TW6 2JA

Telephone: 081 562 1412
Facsimile: 081 759 4314

Ref: CR/940401830/HLE

Dear Mr Ravenscroft

Thank you for your letter of 26 March, concerning your recent journey with us.

Baggage allowances vary considerably depending upon geographical area. Regrettably, you have omitted your travel details from your letter, therefore, I do not know your destination. The United States and Canada operate a '2 piece' system for journeys into and out of their countries, whereas the general rule elsewhere in the world is a single piece limited by weight.

We will not usually weigh a passenger's luggage unless it is comprised of more than one piece, or it is abnormally heavy or bulky. An excess charge will be levied for each kilo above the standard allowances of 23 kilos.

We would like to make it clear that an excess baggage charge is not a fine or penalty, but a charge for providing an additional handling service. Liability for excess baggage charges is not related to the number of passengers on a flight or the amount of

British Airways Plc.
Registered office,
Speedbird House
Heathrow Airport (London)
Hounslow TW6 2JA
Registered in England No. 1777777

other passengers' baggage on a flight. The charge for the standard allowance is part of the fare and any passenger exceeding the allowance would have been charged appropriately. I am sure that our check-in agent did not force the gentleman in question to consume the chocolate that he removed from his baggage.

We are nevertheless sorry for the problems you experienced on this occasion and hope that you have not been deterred from using our services again in the future.

Yours sincerely

Hedy Beecham
Customer Relations Executive

The Elms
Wenter Road
New Mills
High Peak
Derbyshire

The Chairman
British Airways PLC
Speedbird House
PO Box 10
Heathrow Airport
Hounslow
Middlesex
TW6 2JA

25th April

Dear Chairman

I enclose copies of a letter of complaint which I recently wrote to British Airways, and the reply that I received. I suggest that you familiarise yourself with the contents of this correspondence before continuing.

I have never in my life read such an evasive letter as BA's reply. It does not even attempt to address any of the three points which I raised. And it certainly doesn't address the matter of my ruined Hush Puppies! All it does is waffle on about what is or is not excess baggage, which has nothing to do with anything.

It seems to me that at least one member of your staff is still adopting the same cavalier attitude to business as BA did before it caught a cold with the Virgin Atlantic 'dirty tricks' disgrace. Might I say that if BA continue to treat my complaint in this manner that I will have no alternative but to seek satisfaction in some other way.

Yours faithfully

T Ravenscroft (Mr)

BRITISH AIRWAYS

Customer Relations

11th May

British Airways Plc
PO Box 10 (S506)
Heathrow Airport
Hounslow
Middlesex TW6 2JA

Telephone: 081 562 1412
Facsimile: 081 759 4314

Mr T Ravenscroft
The Elms
Wenter Road
New Mills
High Peak
Derbyshire

Dear Mr Ravenscroft

Thank you for your letter of 25 April, from which I regret you remain disappointed following recent correspondence with our Customer Relations department. Please accept my apologies on that account.

At the outset, I should explain that our staff would not normally raise an issue about excess baggage charges for one kilogram. That said, however, the response you received from Customer Relations gave the basic details of baggage allowances and when charges are made.

With regard to the incident during the flight, I was sorry to note that your shoes were ruined. If you would be kind enough, therefore, to let my Executive Assistant at the above address have the details of the cost of replacement, he will arrange for an appropriate refund to be made.

Yours sincerely

Barbara Brooks
Executive Assistant to Sir Colin Marshall

British Airways Plc,
Registered office:
Speedbird House
Heathrow Airport (London)
Hounslow TW6 2JA
Registered in England No. 1777777

The Elms
Wenter Road
New Mills
High Peak
Derbyshire

Executive Assistant to Sir Colin Marshall
British Airways PO Box 10   12th May
Heathrow Airport
Hounslow
Middlesex
TW6 2JA

Dear Executive Assistant

Reference the letter dated 11th May which I received from Sir Colin Marshall.

Firstly would you pass on my thanks to Sir Colin for the efficient way in which he has dealt with this unpleasant matter. With a man like Sir Colin at the helm, or should I say joystick, British Airways will soon be up there with Air France and Lufthansa.

The cost of the replacement of my Hush Puppies is £44. However I am a man of some means to whom money means very little. That doesn't mean to say however that British Airways should go unpunished for the incident. Therefore I would be grateful if instead of sending the money to me you would make a donation to Cancer Research. I look forward to travelling with British Airways many times in the future.

Yours faithfully

T Ravenscroft (Mr)

BRITISH AIRWAYS

Customer Relations

26th May

Mr T Ravenscroft
The Elms
Wenter Road
New Mills
High Peak
Derbyshire

British Airways Plc
PO Box 10 (S506)
Heathrow Airport
Hounslow
Middlesex TW6 2JA

Telephone: 081 562 1412
Facsimile: 081 759 4314

Dear Mr Ravenscroft

Thank you for your letter of 12 May.

As requested, I have arranged for a donation of £44.00 to be made to Cancer Research, and I enclose a copy of my letter to them for your information.

I have also passed on your kind remarks to Sir Colin, and I hope that we can look forward to welcoming you on board one of our flights again soon.

Yours sincerely

Barbara Brooks
Executive Assistant
Enc

END OF CORRESPONDENCE

British Airways Plc.
Registered office.
Speedbird House
Heathrow Airport (London)
Hounslow TW6 2JA
Registered in England No. 1777777

The Elms
Wenter Road
New Mills
High Peak
Derbyshire

Air Malta
314-316 Upper Richmond Road   5th April
Putney
LONDON
SW15 6TU

Dear Air Malta

I hope to visit Malta for a holiday later this year, and with this in mind I am looking for an airline which can cater for my special dietary needs during the flight.

My problem is that I live largely on a diet of stir-fried mulberry leaves. I say largely, what I mean exactly is that I can eat more or less anything I want within reason, just so long as I eat a generous helping of stir-fried mulberry leaves at the same time. This is because for the past three years I have suffered from a rare medical condition, which renders me allergic to all food, unless its effect on my digestive system is neutralised by hot mulberry leaves. (Cold mulberry leaves won't do, they have to be hot and fresh, which is why stir-frying is the best cooking medium.)

I have already approached a couple of airlines and informed them of my special requirements, but without success. The excuse in both cases was that they couldn't guarantee being able to obtain the mulberry leaves. However since then I have had a flash of inspiration. Why don't I bring along my own mulberry leaves! All that will then be required is for you to stir-fry them for me. I realise of course that you aren't a Chinese airline, but Chinese airlines don't seem to fly to Malta, otherwise I would have asked one of them.

However Maltese people do look a bit Chinese, so I'm sure that one of your cabin crew should be able to handle a wok, if they can spare a few minutes from going around with the duty-frees.

I look forward to hearing from you.

Yours faithfully

T Ravenscroft (Mr)

AIR MALTA

Air Malta Company Limited
Air Malta House
314/316 Upper Richmond Rd.,
Putney, London SW15 6TU
Telephone: 081-785 3199 (3 lines)
Telex: 923213 MALMOV
Telefax: 081-785 7468

Mr T Ravenscroft
The Elms
Wenter Road
New Mills
High Peak
Derbyshire

19th April

Dear Mr Ravenscroft

I am in receipt of your letter dated 5th April.

I can appreciate that your medical condition presents you with a travelling predicament since many airlines, including Air Malta, would not be able to cater for such dietary needs. Air Malta can only reheat cooked food and would not carry out any type of cooking during the flight.

Assuring you of our best attention at all times.

Yours sincerely

Edward Kelly
Reservations Supervisor

The Elms
Wenter Road
New Mills
High Peak
Derbyshire

Edward Kelly
Reservations Supervisor Air Malta   23rd April
314-316 Upper Richmond Road
LONDON
SW15 6TU

Dear Mr Kelly

Reference your letter dated 19th April.

If I pre-cooked the mulberry leaves would Air Malta be able to heat them up for me? If so, things should be just fine, because even in the event that they were served up a little less than piping hot there is only a fifty per cent chance that I would suffer a reaction, according to my doctor.

What happens to me when I do get a reaction is that my digestive system goes berserk, with the result that my eyes glaze over and I babble loud gibberish for up to thirty minutes. (A friend of mine wittily refers to this as my John Prescott impression.) However, as long as the passengers seated in the dozen or so rows in the immediate vicinity are aware of the situation everything should be hunky-dory. Or you could lock me in one of the lavatories for half an hour, I wouldn't mind. In fact I wouldn't even know about it until I emerged from my fit, and then, due to my digestive system being on the blink, a lavatory is where I need to be anyway.

I do hope that you will be able to accommodate me.

Yours sincerely

T Ravenscroft (Mr)

AIR MALTA

Air Malta Company Limited
Air Malta House
314/316 Upper Richmond Rd.,
Putney, London SW15 6TU
Telephone: 081-785 3199 (3 lines)
Telex: 923213 MALMOV
Telefax: 081-785 7468

Mr T Ravenscroft
The Elms
Wenter Road
New Mills
High Peak
Derbyshire

19th May

Dear Mr Ravenscroft

I am in receipt of your letter dated 12 May.

I understand from the attached copy of a letter dated 23 April, that there is always a possibility, however small, that you may suffer a reaction during a flight.

Going by your own description of how you would behave if you were to get a reaction during a flight, it is clear that Air Malta would not be able to fully guarantee your well-being nor the well-being of other passengers on the same flight.

Your reactionary in-flight behaviour would certainly present health & safety problems to the cabin crew and the Airline would never accept such risks, however remote.

Assuring you of my best attention at all times.

Yours sincerely

Edward Kelly
Reservations Supervisor

The Elms
Wenter Road
New Mills
High Peak
Derbyshire

Edward Kelly
Reservations Supervisor Air Malta   24th May
314-316 Upper Richmond Road
LONDON
SW15 6TU

Dear Mr Kelly

Reference your letter dated 19th May.

I am very perturbed with this reply, to say the least. I am sure I don't have to remind you that it was the island of Malta which controlled the vital sea lanes between Italy and Africa during World War Two, thanks largely to the fighter aircraft 'Faith, Hope and Charity', and which resulted in your country being awarded the George Cross. It would appear that the crew of these aeroplanes were made of sterner stuff than the crews employed by Air Malta, since they coped with everything that the German war machine could throw at them, whereas your Air Malta crews apparently can't cope with one demented (possibly) passenger.

I would respectfully point out to you that had it not been for the Royal Air Force there would probably not now be a Malta to fly to, and that in future you would do well to bear this in mind when dealing with British passengers, from whom no request should be too difficult for you.

Yours sincerely

T Ravenscroft (Mr)   END OF CORRESPONDENCE

The Elms
Wenter Road
New Mills
High Peak
Derbyshire

Virgin Atlantic Airways Ltd
Sussex House   31st March
Crawley
RH10 1DQ

Dear Virgin Atlantic Airways

I recently travelled with your airline to the States, and an otherwise top-class flight both getting there and coming back was spoiled by the mediocrity of the in-flight movies. I realise of course that with children on board you cannot show films like 'Emmanuelle' and 'Friday the Thirteenth' nor would I want to see such films, but to inflict such dross as 'Sister Act' on paying passengers is taking blandness a little too far.

Bearing the above in mind I have a suggestion to make to you. I am a founder member of the 'New Mills Players', a very successful amateur (although very 'professional' in performance) drama society. We have recently diversified into making films and have two 'in the can' already. They are 'Lady Don't Look Backwards', the story of an aristocratic lady who falls from grace, and 'Continental Shift', a French factory saga set in the sixties, which is very much influenced by Zola in its portrayal of French low-life, and by Bunuel in its imagery. Both these films are full-length and shot on video. Currently in production is 'Hitler's List', an in-depth condemnation of the Nazi war machine and its infamous Fuehrer. At a running time of four hours and thirty minutes 'Hitler's List' will be even longer than 'Schindler's List', but then Hitler had a longer list.

All our films are suitable for a family audience, and far superior quality-wise to any film I have seen on the three trips to the

States I have made with you during the last twelve months. The price of the films is £5000 each. This price gives you at Virgin Atlantic exclusive 'in the air' rights to the films, and as many prints as you have aeroplanes. When word gets round that you are showing the films it will doubtless pull in many extra passengers so you will recoup your expenditure on the films very quickly indeed.

I await your order.

Yours sincerely

T Ravenscroft (Mr)

Virgin Atlantic Airways Ltd., 2nd Floor, Griffin House, High Street, Crawley, West Sussex RH10 1DQ
Customer Relations Tel: 0293 · 616161 Fax: 0293 · 561713 Baggage Systems and Procedures Tel: 0293 · 616161 Fax: 0293 · 561713

Ref : JS/039712/1/RAV

14 April

Mr T Ravenscroft
The Elms
Wenter Road
New Mills
High Peak
Derbyshire

Dear Mr Ravenscroft

Many thanks for your recent kind letter to Virgin Atlantic.

Normally our Customer Relations staff reply immediately, however, on this occasion, please accept our apologies for the delay. You can be assured that it is receiving our attention.

Thank you for your patience.

Kind regards

Maria Adams (Mrs)
Customer Relations

Registered Office: 120 Campden Hill Road, London W8 7AR. Registered in England 1600117. VAT Number: GB.426-2161-84

The Elms
Wenter Road
New Mills
High Peak
Derbyshire

Lord Richard Branson
Virgin Atlantic Airways Ltd   1st May
2nd Floor
Griffin House
High Street
Crawley
West Sussex
RH10 1DQ

Dear Lord Richard

I enclose a copy of a letter which I sent to Virgin Atlantic on the 31st of March. On the 14th of April your Customer Relations Department acknowledged the letter and promised that the matter was receiving attention. All I can say is that it isn't receiving all that much attention, because it is now the 1st of May and the matter still hasn't been dealt with. In fact if you personally had received as much attention from prospective clients when you were trying to get Branson's Pickles up and running you would still be in the starting blocks. And I think it is safe to say that if you had failed with Branson's Pickles you would certainly have failed when it came to launching Virgin Atlantic, and as for your hot-air balloon it would never have got off the ground, far less round the world.

What I am saying Lord Richard is that if people are not given a chance then they can never succeed, and your company is not giving the New Mills Players and me a chance. Great oaks from little acorns grow – but only if they're planted.

Yours faithfully

T Ravenscroft (Mr)

The Elms
Wenter Road
New Mills
High Peak
Derbyshire

Lord Richard Branson
Virgin Atlantic Airways Ltd
2nd Floor
Griffin House
High Street
Crawley
West Sussex
RH10 1DQ

26th May

Dear Lord Richard

You still have to reply to my letter of 31st March, despite my reminding you in a further letter on 1st May. If this is an example of your business expertise no wonder you didn't get the concession for the National Lottery.

I have bought my last jar of your pickles. They're not half as good as PanYan anyway.

Yours faithfully

T Ravenscroft (Mr)

Virgin Atlantic Airways Ltd., 2nd Floor, Griffin House, High Street, Crawley, West Sussex RH10 1DQ
Customer Relations Tel: 0293 · 616161 Fax: 0293 · 561713 Baggage Systems and Procedures Tel: 0293 · 616161 Fax: 0293 · 561713

26 May

Mr T Ravenscroft
The Elms
Wenter Road
New Mills
High Peak
Derbyshire

Dear Mr Ravenscroft

I am sorry for the delay in replying to your letter to Richard Branson.

I am also sorry that you did not enjoy the movies on your recent flight. We regularly win awards for our programming and our movies consist of a mixture of current blockbusters, arthouse films and classics. We try and provide something for everyone, so of course I am disappointed that you couldn't find anything to enjoy.

I am loathe to change what has proved to be a successful mix, so I regret we would not be able to purchase your movies. They are also very expensive. A movie like the Oscar winning "Philadelphia" we are currently screening, costs us $3,000 for two months.

Thanks for taking the time to write.

Yours sincerely

Lysette Morris
Inflight Entertainment Executive.

Registered Office: 120 Campden Hill Road, London W8 7AR. Registered in England 1600117. VAT Number: GB.425-2161-84

The Elms
Wenter Road
New Mills
High Peak
Derbyshire

Lysette Morris
Inflight Entertainment Executive   31st May
Virgin Atlantic Airways Ltd
2nd Floor
Griffin House
High Street
Crawley
West Sussex
RH10 1DQ

Dear Lysette Morris

Thank you for your letter of 26th May. I have already written to Lord Richard Branson about the dilatory way his company is run, so he will no doubt be making a few staff changes. I would suggest that if you don't jettison your prejudices and adopt a more enlightened film-buying policy, and generally pull your socks up, that it will be in the post of Inflight Entertainment Executive that one of the first changes will be made.

To compare the boring if worthy 'Philadelphia' with the benchmark films which the New Mills Players are turning out is an insult to a dedicated and very talented group of thespians. Granted Tom Hanks wasn't bad in the role of the brown hatter with Aids, but his performance pales into insignificance when compared to that of our vicar, in a similar role, in the New Mills Players' forthcoming Anglo-Indian epic 'Bite My Pilau'. Although it must be conceded that as the vicar isn't exactly averse to rogering the odd choirboy or three he isn't exactly acting.

Furthermore our films are not, as you try to claim, expensive. You are failing to take into account the fact that the price gives you exclusive 'in the air' rights. This can only lead to an increase in passengers, once the word gets around that the only place you can see these magnificent films is on a Virgin Atlantic aeroplane.

However, as an inducement, I am able to offer you any two of 'Lady Don't Look Backwards', 'Hitler's List', 'Bite My Pilau' or our new James Bond film 'Stockport Is Too Much' featuring Dr GoldnoJaws and his oriental assistant Blow Job for the bargain price of £8000. I will also throw in a product placement of a jar of Branson's Pickles in 'Bite My Pilau', on the table of an Indian restaurant on which the vicar is making love to his friend Ravi Shankhim.

If you take me up on this offer it could well save you your job.

Yours sincerely

T Ravenscroft (Mr)
Copy to – Lord Richard Branson

Virgin Atlantic Airways Ltd., 2nd Floor, Griffin House, High Street, Crawley, West Sussex RH10 1DQ
Customer Relations Tel: 0293 · 616161 Fax: 0293 · 561713 Baggage Systems and Procedures Tel: 0293 · 616161 Fax: 0293 · 561713

8 July

Mr T Ravenscroft
The Elms
Wenter Road
New Mills
High Peak
Derbyshire

Dear Mr Ravenscroft

If you would care to send me some viewing cassettes of the movies you would like us to consider for inflight use, I would be interested to take a look at them.

Yours sincerely

Lysette Morris
Inflight Entertainment Executive.

END OF CORRESPONDENCE

Registered Office: 120 Campden Hill Road, London W8 7AR. Registered in England 1600117. VAT Number: GB.425-2161-84

The Elms
Wenter Road
New Mills
High Peak
Derbyshire

SAS Scandinavian Airlines
52 Conduit Street   30th March
LONDON
W1R 0AY

Dear SAS

I have not flown for some years as nowadays what with hijacks
and bombs exploding in mid-air I consider it to be far too
dangerous.

This has obviously limited my choice of holiday destination,
not least because my wife is a notoriously bad sailor, and the
Isle of Man ferry is about all that she can handle – and even
then I have to get her drunk before boarding her!

Imagine my joy then when I learned that the SAS ran an
airline. I will certainly have no qualms about our aeroplane
being hijacked or blown out of the skies if you 'Who Dares
Wins' boys are running the show! I for one will never forget
the way you dealt with those terrorists at that Middle East
Embassy in London a few years back, not to mention your
heroism in the Falklands conflict. By the way, is the
'Scandinavian' bit in your name a cover? I suppose so.

I don't know which destinations you fly to so if you could let
me know them as soon as possible my wife and I can start to
make our holiday arrangements.

Yours faithfully

T Ravenscroft (Mr)

The Travel Book

March 27 – June 25

*Your guide to
SAS travel services
including business hotels
and*

SAS Worldwide Timetable

////// SAS

The Elms
Wenter Road
New Mills
High Peak
Derbyshire

SAS Scandinavian Airlines
52 Conduit Street   6th April
LONDON
W1R 0AY

Dear SAS

Thank you for your guide to SAS Travel Services which you
kindly and promptly sent to me following my letter of the
30th March.

Since writing to you I happened to see an advertisement for
SAS in a magazine, and was more than a little surprised to
learn that you employ stewardesses on your aeroplanes.
Frankly I didn't realise that the SAS employed females – I
thought your force was made up entirely of macho males who
look like Martin Shaw. On reflection though I don't suppose
there is any reason why you shouldn't employ members of the
fairer sex, after all my wife packs a fair punch, especially when
she's been at the bottle.

It also causes me some concern that your stewardesses don't
wear the normal SAS uniform when on the aeroplane. How
then are potential hijackers to know that they are dealing with
the SAS, and therefore have second thoughts on hijacking the
aeroplane, if they can't recognise you by your SAS uniform?
Attractive as your girls look in their uniforms I do think that
your normal gear of black sweater, black trousers, hard helmet
and riot shield would give your passengers more confidence
that the aeroplane isn't suddenly going to be commandeered
by some Middle East fanatic.

Incidentally, are your stewardesses' uniforms for sale, as I would
like one for my wife? I'm trying to get one from Air UK but

there is a possibility they might let me down, but yours are almost as attractive and if I end up with two that will mean twice as much fun, won't it.

Finally, and despite the reservations outlined above, I have decided to fly SAS to Australia, first class, the first week in September, returning one month later. I will be taking my wife and six children, aged fifteen months to sixteen years, and I would appreciate it if you could write to me giving the price of the tickets and where I can purchase them.

Yours faithfully

T Ravenscroft (Mr)

Singapore Airlines
580 Chiswick High Road
LONDON
W4 5RB

31st March

Dear Singapore Airlines

I have heard that your catering is probably the best in the air, and for this reason I have decided to fly with your airline when I visit Sydney, Australia, this autumn.

En route to Sydney it is my intention to make a stopover in Singapore for a few days. In fact this is the reason I am writing to you, because since deciding on the trip I read something in my newspaper about Malaysia which disturbed me more than somewhat. For the article in my *Daily Telegraph* informed me that it is common practice over there to flog wrongdoers with a cane, and went on to relate the story of the sorry plight of a young American, whom the Malaysian authorities flogged senseless because he had been found guilty of the crime of writing graffiti on motor cars.

Now don't get me wrong, I have no intention of writing graffiti, or for that matter committing any other crime, whilst I am in your country, but it is possible even in the most just of societies to be wrongly accused and convicted of a crime. Then again, what exactly is classified as a crime in Singapore? I have heard that you are hot on litter louts over there, so what for example would the position be if I happened to be kidnapped during my stay in Singapore, wrote a 'Help!' note which I somehow managed to throw onto the pavement, and the note was subsequently found and I was rescued? Quite naturally I would expect the kidnappers to be given very short shrift, but how would I stand with regard to causing the 'help' note to be on the pavement – could I be flogged for the crime of dropping litter?

Sampling the delights which Singapore no doubt has to offer is all very well, but not at the expense of having a bottom that I wouldn't be able to sit down on for a month! Or is the dropping of litter not a floggable offence?

I would be very grateful if you could let me know because it may mean the difference between my stopping over in Singapore or flying direct to Australia – still with Singapore Airlines of course.

Yours faithfully

T Ravenscroft (Mr)

Mr T Ravenscroft
The Elms
Wenter Road
New Mills
High Peak
Derbyshire

MANS2632
13th April

Dear Mr Ravenscroft

I refer to your letter addressed to our London office regarding your concern over crime punishment in Singapore.

Your comments are understandable, but your fears are groundless. The penalty for dropping litter in Singapore is a fixed fine of S$500. I have yet to hear of anybody being jailed for this offence, let alone flogging.

Your example of the American youth being flogged was for a series of serious offences which necessitated bringing the matter to public light that such crimes would not be tolerated by Singapore nationals or overseas residents.

I can honestly state that during my frequent visits to Singapore, over the last 20 years that I have been employed by Singapore Airlines, I have never encountered any incident which was unfairly dealt with by the authorities.

I strongly recommend that you take the advantage of a stopover in Singapore enroute to Sydney. It has a lot to offer.

If you have any further doubts, please do not hesitate to give me a call on ▬▬▬▬▬▬▬.

Yours sincerely

JIM BELCH
SALES MANAGER NORTHERN ENGLAND

Macintosh House • Market Place • Shambles Square • Manchester M4 3AF
Telephone Reservations 061-832 3346 • Administration 061-832 6929

Incorporated in Singapore

The Elms
Wenter Road
New Mills
High Peak
Derbyshire

Jim Belch
Singapore Airlines Ltd   25th April
Macintosh House
Market Place
Shambles Square
MANCHESTER
M4 3AF

Dear Mr Belch

Reference your letter to me dated 13th April. I was almost reassured by your letter, but finally common sense prevailed. Penalties for crimes are continually changing to suit the prevailing mood of society, and whereas in Singapore today's punishment for dropping litter is $500, tomorrow's punishment might be a flogging to within an inch of one's life.

I have always gone along with the view that there is no smoke without fire, so just as long as there is even the slightest possibility of the smoke and fire in question emanating from my buttocks, through them being thoroughly flogged, I am afraid I will have to forsake the pleasures of Singapore.

Or perhaps there is a non-buttock-beating country I could touch down in for a few days whilst on my way to Australia with Singapore Airlines?

Yours sincerely

T Ravenscroft (Mr)

SINGAPORE AIRLINES LIMITED

Mr T Ravenscroft
The Elms
Wenter Road
New Mills
High Peak
Derbyshire

MANS2655
28th April

Dear Mr Ravenscroft

I refer to your letter dated 25 April.

I am sorry you still do not feel confident in having a stopover in Singapore enroute to Australia.

Regrettably, I cannot think of any safer place to stopover, or suggest any place on the way that I can guarantee will offer a similar laxed attitude to punishment as found in the UK. Under the circumstances I can only recommend you travel straight through to Australia.

Please do not hesitate to phone me should you wish more clarification.

Yours sincerely

JIM BELCH
SALES MANAGER NORTHERN ENGLAND

END OF CORRESPONDENCE

Macintosh House • Market Place • Shambles Square • Manchester M4 3AF
Telephone Reservations 061-832 3346 • Administration 061-832 6929

Incorporated in Singapore

The Elms
Wenter Road
New Mills
High Peak
Derbyshire

Air France
100 Hammersmith Road   30th March
LONDON
W6 7JP

Dear Air France

I recently travelled with your airline to Paris Charles de Gaulle
and had a most pleasant flight, both going there and coming
back, as is usually the case with Air France. Quite superb in-
flight croissants it goes without saying. However the happy
memories of the trip have since been somewhat marred. This
is because of the preferential treatment you gave to a passenger
with a broken leg on the return journey, allowing him to board
the aeroplane before the other passengers, and allocating him
a privileged seat. Because this passenger did not have a broken
leg! I know this for a fact because the man in question is a
member of my golf club, and two days after the flight he was
walking round the golf course like a two-year-old!

I brought up with him the subject of his 'broken leg' and he
just laughed and told me that whenever he flies he always
pretends that he has a broken leg so that he will receive
preferential treatment. Words failed me!

After thinking it over I feel that something must be done about
the matter, as this man flies regularly to Paris on business, and
I can simply not stomach the thought of the bounder
continually duping you like this. Not to mention his getting
better treatment than his fellow passengers, who have paid
exactly the same price.

I feel that I should blow the gaff on this man without further ado, but I will leave the final decision to you. So please let me know as soon as possible if you wish me to reveal the name of the culprit.

Yours faithfully

T Ravenscroft (Mr)

Mr T Ravenscroft
The Elms
Wenter Road
New Mills
High Peak
Derbyshire

LONSL/94/4569/27/ca
April 12

Dear Mr Ravenscroft

We refer to your letter of 30th March and thank you for your complimentary comments regarding our services when you travelled aboard our services from Charles de Gaulle.

We have noted your comments regarding a fellow passenger who presented himself as having a broken leg in order to receive preferential treatment and we thank you for bringing this matter to our attention.

We are sending a copy of our letter to our Passenger Handling Manager to our London Heathrow Airport office, who we are sure will be interested in its contents.

Yours sincerely

AIR FRANCE
Cathleen Acham
Customer Relations Department

Colet Court 100 Hammersmith Road London W6 7JP
Telephone Reservations 081 742 6600
Other Departments 081 759 2311
Fax Reservations Services Ticket Office
Passenger Sales Department 081 750 4488
All other Departments 081 750 4391
Contact Telephone No

Compagnie Nationale Air France Incorporated in France

The Elms
Wenter Road
New Mills
High Peak
Derbyshire

Cathleen Acham
Customer Relations Department   16th April
100 Hammersmith Road
LONDON
W6 7JP

Dear Cathleen Acham

Thank you for your letter of 12th April.

Actually, in the time between my sending my letter and receiving your reply there has been a development, and consequently I will not be able to reveal to Air France the name of the bounder who keeps duping your airline. This is because I had an altercation with him at the golf club – he was trying to cheat by dropping his balls in the rough – and I ended up telling him of my intention to denounce him to you. Unfortunately I wasn't aware that the man in question knew about the 'arrangement' I have with the barmaid at the golf club, and he threatened that if I blew the whistle reference the broken leg incident he would tell my wife about my little indiscretion (sadly English wives aren't as understanding of a man's needs as French wives, more's the pity, and if my wife ever found out about 'mon affaire' my life wouldn't be worth living).

However, the whole business got me thinking, and it occurred to me that other passengers may also be getting preferential treatment by pretending that they have broken legs. The more I think about it the more likely it seems – certainly it seems that every time I pass through an airport departure lounge I see at least a couple of broken legs, a far higher proportion than I see if I go anywhere else – and they can't all be skiing accidents as I see as many broken legs departing the country as I do arriving in it.

I therefore have a proposition which I would like to put to you, since I am sure that you will wish to stamp out this sorry business. On receiving a request for preferential treatment due to a broken leg, Air France will pass on to me the name of the applicant. I will then pay the man a visit. If he does have a broken leg, all well and good, but if he doesn't I will do one of two things, depending upon how seriously you at Air France view the matter. I will either:-

(a) Tell him that his little game is up, or

(b) Break his leg.

I would charge a nominal fee of £10 per passenger for this service, plus expenses. I await your reply with interest.

Yours faithfully

T Ravenscroft (Mr)

The Elms
Wenter Road
New Mills
High Peak
Derbyshire

Aer Lingus Plc
Dublin Airport   31st March
DUBLIN
Ireland

Dear Aer Lingus

Travelling with your airline recently I asked one of your charming stewardesses, Bridget I think her name was, what the 'Lingus' in the name Aer Lingus meant. Unfortunately she didn't know, nor did any of your cabin crew.

When I arrived home I looked up the word in my dictionary, or rather I didn't look it up, as there was no entry for Lingus in my Concise Oxford. I thought for a moment that it might be a suffix, but quickly discarded that idea as I only know one word which has Lingus as a suffix, and it can't possibly mean that, because although Aer Lingus is by no means the most impressive airline that I have ever flown with, it certainly doesn't suck.

Could it perhaps be a Gaelic word? Maybe someone there at HQ knows its origin? If so I would be very grateful if you could pass it on to me as not knowing the meaning of it is driving me to distraction.

Yours sincerely

T Ravenscroft (Mr)

Aer Lingus ❧

Dublin Airport, Dublin, Ireland

Telephone: Head Office 01-705 2222
General Fax 01-705 3832
Telegrams/Telex: Dublin 31404

Direct Telephone Number

Direct Fax Number

Mr T Ravenscroft
The Elms
Wenter Road
New Mills
High Peak
Derbyshire

19th April

Dear Mr Ravenscroft

Thank you for your recent letter.

There's a very simple answer to your question. 'Aer Lingus' is an Irish phrase meaning, appropriately enough, air fleet. Initially in 1936, the company operated under the name 'Irish Sea Airways', but this was soon changed to Aer Lingus, which we have been operating under ever since.

I hope you didn't lose too much sleep over this and thank you for your interest in Aer Lingus.

Yours sincerely

Yvonne Bolger
Aer Lingus Group Corporate Affairs

Directors: B M Cahill (Chairman), M Bennett, P Kavanagh, R P Manson, J Malone, M Rafferty, D Sweeney, E Whelan, S Whelan, P Wright.
Aer Lingus plc - Member of IATA. Registration: Ireland 9215. Registered Office: Dublin Airport, Ireland.

The Elms
Wenter Road
New Mills
High Peak
Derbyshire

Yvonne Bolger
Aer Lingus Plc   24th April
Dublin Airport
DUBLIN
Ireland

Dear Yvonne Bolger

Thank you for your letter of 19th April.

I assume that you changed the name of your airline from Irish
Sea Airways to Aer Lingus because you wanted to give it an Irish
flavour. However Aer Lingus, which I am assuming is Gaelic,
only makes sense to someone who speaks this obscure language.
If you want to highlight the 'Irishness' of your airline, while at
the same time making the name understandable to anyone who
speaks English, the perfect appellation for it would be Aer
O'Plane.

You have my permission to use this name if you wish, free of
charge.

Yours sincerely

T Ravenscroft (Mr)

Olympic Airlines
11 Conduit Street
LONDON
W1R 0LB

24th April

Dear Olympic Airlines

I will be flying to Crete with your airline in July, and on my return journey will be bringing back with me an item of masonry. The piece in question is a large stone urn which is at the moment, according to a photograph in the 'Go Greek' travel brochure, in a place called Knossos, which I gather is an ancient Minoan city. I don't know too much about Minoans but they certainly knew how to make an attractive urn! It looks quite splendid next to the olive tree outside the doorway of what I suppose was a Minoan nobleman's house, but I assure you that it will look even nicer in my garden, next to the rhododendron bushes. I don't suppose you will miss it, as you seem to have lots of similar ones in Greece, even if most of them are broken.

I would estimate the weight of the urn to be about fifty kilograms, so could you let me know how much I will have to pay to bring it back to England with me on the aeroplane?

Looking forward to hearing from you.

Yours sincerely

T Ravenscroft (Mr)

OLYMPIC AIRWAYS

11 CONDUIT STREET
LONDON W1R 0LP
Tel: 071-409 2400
Fax: 071-493 0563

Date as postmark

Your reference

Our reference   LONSC9649

Dear Sir/Madam
~~XXXXX~~
Thank you for your communication dated   5th April. Kindly contact
our Cargo Department and they should
be able to answer any questions you may have.
Yours faithfully   Assuring you of our closest attention.

Customer Relations
OA - London

END OF CORRESPONDENCE

117

The Elms
Wenter Road
New Mills
High Peak
Derbyshire

Qantas Airway
Qantas House
395 King Street   7th April
Hammersmith
LONDON
W6 9NJ

Dear Qantas Airways

My wife and I and six children will be visiting Australia for
the first time in September. At the moment I can't make up
my mind whether we should fly British Airways, as we usually
do, or fly with an Australian airline, which might perhaps
allow us to get 'a taste of Australia' before we actually arrive
in your country.

With this in mind, what does your airline offer that can be
said to be typically antipodean? I'm not expecting the
Captain to have three legs and look like Rolf Harris, or the
stewardesses to look like Kylie Minogue or anything like
that, but maybe the food you serve during the flight is
typically Australian? (Although I will skip the Australian
wine if it's all the same to you, for despite all the good press
it has had recently it still tastes like methylated blackcurrant
jam to me.) Or maybe the in-flight movies are Australian? I
missed the one about the dingo that ate the baby when it
was on at our local cinema, so a chance to see it would be
most welcome.

Incidentally, bearing the above in mind, at what age would
you say that a baby is safe from being swallowed by a dingo?
You see my youngest will only be fifteen months old come

September, and I would rather leave him safe in Sydney with my wife when the children and I visit the Ayers Rock area than risk him becoming a dingo's dinner.

Looking forward to hearing from you.

Yours faithfully

T Ravenscroft (Mr)

QANTAS

Qantas Airways Limited
A.C.N. 009 661 901

395/403 King Street
London. W6 9NJ

Telephone:
Administration: 081 846 046
Reservations:
                Linkline 0345-74776
Fax: 061 746 8551

Mr T Ravenscroft
The Elms
Wenter Road
New Mills
High Peak
Derbyshire

11 April

Our ref: GEN/D167-94/ZH

Dear Mr Ravenscroft

Further to your recent letter dated 7th April, I have pleasure in enclosing various items of literature to help you plan your proposed journey with Qantas Airways.

Should you require any further information our reservations staff will be happy to help with any queries you may have. Their linkline number is ▮▮▮▮▮▮▮▮▮▮▮. Our staff can also assist you should you wish to hold a provisional reservation and can also offer services such as hotel booking and car hire.

Alternatively, if I can be of any further assistance, please feel free to contact me at any time quoting the above reference number.

Yours sincerely

Zoe Horner (Miss)
RESERVATIONS SERVICES DEPARTMENT
ENCS

Zoe Horner
Reservations Services Dept
Qantas Airways Ltd
395/403 King Street
LONDON
W6 9NJ

The Elms
Wenter Road
New Mills
High Peak
Derbyshire

15th April

Dear Miss Horner

Thank you for your prompt reply and for all the information about Qantas. You appear to be a first-class airline, and you can rest assured that my family and I will be flying Qantas come September.

Thank you also for the 'Australia – A Traveller's Guide', which was packed with information about the many delights awaiting us in 'Oz'. Having all read the guide my family can hardly wait until September, especially Jeremy, my eldest. I overheard him talking to one of his friends, and he mentioned that once he hits Bondo Beach he's going to get down to some serious bushbuzzing, whatever that is.

Useful as the guide is however, it didn't contain the one piece of information which I consider to be vital if I am to have peace of mind whilst I am in your country. For, despite many references to Ayers Rock, the guide didn't once mention dingoes – in fact I can't find the word 'dingo' in any of the guide's 128 pages. Still, I suppose that after all the publicity about the Lindy Chamberlain case, which couldn't have done your tourist industry any good at all, that you prefer to let sleeping dogs lie. However the trouble is that your dogs don't lie and sleep, they cruise around looking for babies to eat, which is why I am writing to you again. In my original letter I asked you at what age you would consider a baby to be safe from death by dingo. To help you to help me I have measured and weighed my next-door-neighbour's son, who is now exactly the same age as my youngest will be come September. He stands twenty-five inches tall and scales twenty-six pounds. Given this information, do you think my youngest will be safe?

Hope to hear from you soon.

Yours faithfully

T Ravenscroft (Mr)

PS. In both the Qantas literature and the 'Australia – A Traveller's Guide', frequent reference is made to 'Australia's fine wines'. Frankly I find Australian wine to be the most frightful stuff, as do many people in this country who can recognise a decent bottle. And if people were to get the impression that you are being less than honest about your wine........? Enough said.

QANTAS

Qantas Airways Limited
A.C.N. 009 661 901

395/403 King Street
London. W6 9NJ

Telephone:
Administration: 081 846 0466
Reservations:
Linkline 0345-747767

Fax. 081 748 8551

Mr T Ravenscroft
The Elms
Wenter Road
New Mills
High Peak
Derbyshire

21 April

Our ref: GEN/D167-94/ZH

Dear Mr Ravenscroft

Thank you for your recent letter dated 15th April, with respect to
your forthcoming journey to Australia.

As an airline, we hold very limited information about the Australian
wildlife, and unfortunately our literature does not cover your query.
I can only suggest that you contact the Australian Tourist
Commission or a Zoo, who may be able to assist with your question.

I have pleasure in advising some contacts for your query, which I
hope will be useful:
Australian Tourist Commission
1st Floor, Gemini House
10-18 Putney Hill, LONDON
SW15 6AA

Taronga Zoo
Bradleys Head Road
Mosman, NSW 2088
AUSTRALIA

I trust the above information is helpful.

Yours sincerely

Zoe Horner (Miss)
RESERVATIONS SERVICES DEPARTMENT

The Elms
Wenter Road
New Mills
High Peak
Derbyshire

Zoe Horner
Reservations Services Dept   27th April
Qantas Airways Ltd
395/403 King Street
W6 9NJ

Dear Miss Horner

Thank you for your letter dated 21st April.

I am more than a little disappointed that you are unable to help me reference the dingo business, other than to furnish me with a list of organisations in Australia that I could write to. I would have thought that you might have taken a little more trouble to please someone who will shortly be paying your airline over £8000 to fly his family to your country. I am sure you could find out for me the information I require if you really wanted to. You might of course have to tear yourself away from 'Neighbours' or 'Home and Away' for a few minutes, but I'm sure you could manage it if you made the effort.

Yours sincerely

T Ravenscroft (Mr)

QANTAS *CUSTOMER RELATIONS*

OUR REF: GCRLNR00045/94/M

Mr T Ravenscroft
The Elms
Wenter Road
New Mills
High Peak
Derbyshire

April 28

Dear Mr Ravenscroft

I refer to your recent correspondence with our Reservations Department, with respect to your forthcoming journey, which has been brought to our attention.

I was indeed concerned to learn of your dissatisfaction with Ms Horner's reply, dated 21 April. I do believe, however, that she had attempted to address your obvious concerns, by providing you with contact details for those organisations best able to respond. Our staff are not qualified zoologists, and it would be incorrect, and indeed unethical, for them to advise you on matters unrelated to our business concerns.

Qantas Airways Limited
A.C.N. 009 661 901

395/403 King Street
London W6 9NJ
United Kingdom
Tel. (081) 846 0534
(081) 846 0529
Fax. (081) 746 3317

I regret that we are not in the habit of acting as a third party in these matters, and are not about to do so. Nevertheless, I may assure you that I personally have no knowledge of any tourist being subject to attack by a wild dingo. Providing you exercise reasonable care, and ensure that your children are accompanied by a responsible adult, I do not see you encountering any difficulties, particularly in those areas which are much frequented tourist attractions.

I trust that you may have an enjoyable holiday in Australia.

Yours sincerely

Trevor E Bluff
A/CUSTOMER RELATIONS MANAGER
UK & IRELAND

The Elms
Wenter Road
New Mills
High Peak
Derbyshire

Trevor E Bluff
Customer Relations Manager
Qantas Airways Ltd
395/403 King Street
London
W6 9NJ

2nd May

Dear Trev

Thank you for your letter of 27th April.

Please convey my apologies to Ms Horner. The truth is that when I wrote the letter I was having a really bad day. On top of the gas and phone bills dropping through the letter box, my youngest – who I quite often wish would be eaten by a dingo, and may very well be if he doesn't behave himself whilst we are in Australia, even if I have to force-feed a dingo with the little sod – had stuffed my glasses down the back of the settee, and in trying to get them out I broke them and cut my hand.

However, that is no excuse for venting my spleen on one of your employees, who I am sure was doing her best, for an Australian. Perhaps because I tipped her off not to push Australia's diabolical wines I expected her to be especially helpful to me, but I see now that she was already being as helpful as her position allowed her to be. Again, please give my apologies to her.

Incidentally, are wines other than Australian ones served on your airline? And if not, would you have any objections to my bringing along a decent bottle of claret to consume on the journey?

Yours sincerely

T Ravenscroft (Mr)

QANTAS CUSTOMER RELATIONS

OUR REF: GCRLNR00045/94/M

Mr T Ravenscroft
The Elms
Wenter Road
New Mills
High Peak
Derbyshire

May 6

Dear Mr Ravenscroft

Thank you for your recent letter addressed to Mr Bluff who is
currently away from the office. A copy of your letter has
been forwarded to Ms Horner.

Regrettably, we do not permit passengers to bring their own
wine onto the aircraft as it is against Customs regulations.
Qantas serve fine Australian wines onboard in Economy Class.

We look forward to welcoming you and your family onboard
our services in September.

Yours sincerely

Ros Chandler (Mrs)
CUSTOMER RELATIONS EXECUTIVE
UK & IRELAND

Qantas Airways Limited
A.C.N. 009 661 901

395/403 King Street
London W6 9NJ
United Kingdom
Tel: (061) 846 0534
     (081) 646 0529
Fax: (081) 748 3317

The Elms
Wenter Road
New Mills
High Peak
Derbyshire

Ros Chandler (Mrs)
Qantas Airways Ltd   9th May
395/403 King Street
London
W6 9NJ

Dear Ros

Thank you for your prompt reply to my letter to Trev. Good on you!

Unfortunately your letter contains a spelling mistake. You have written 'Qantas serve fine Australian wines onboard in Economy Class.' Should this read 'five Australian wines' or 'nine Australian wines'? My wife has suggested that maybe it isn't a spelling mistake and that you actually do mean 'fine' Australian wines but I told her not to be so silly.

With regard to your statement that Customs regulations do not permit passengers to bring their own wine on board, surely you are mistaken, because in my experience it is possible to buy wines and spirits from airport shops as soon as one has passed into the duty-free area. Perhaps you would care to comment on this?

Yours sincerely

T Ravenscroft (Mr)

OUR REF: GCRLNR00045/94/M

Mr T Ravenscroft
The Elms
Wenter Road
New Mills
High Peak
Derbyshire

May 23

Dear Mr Ravenscroft

Thank you for your letter of 9th May.

You are quite correct that there is no Customs Regulation
forbidding the carriage of alcohol onboard. The requirement
is that the bottle must not be opened prior to departure.

Consequently it is correct that you can consume your own
wine onboard. In practice this is not something we would
encourage or advertise. You will appreciate that while the
crew serves the alcohol on board, they are more able to
control the amount consumed.

I hope this clarifies the situation and apologise for our
previous error.

Yours sincerely

Michael Foreman
CUSTOMER RELATIONS DEPARTMENT
UK & IRELAND

Qantas Airways Limited
A.C.N. 009 661 901

395/403 King Street
London W6 9NJ
United Kingdom
Tel: (081) 846 0534
(081) 846 0529
Fax. (081) 746 3317

Michael Foreman
Qantas Airways Ltd
395/403 King Street
London
W6 9NJ

The Elms
Wenter Road
New Mills
High Peak
Derbyshire

24th May

Dear Mr Foreman

Thank you for your letter of 23rd May.

There is only one thing wrong with the Qantas tenet of trying to control the amount of alcohol consumed by its passengers, and that is that the alcohol it serves, leastwise as far as wine is concerned, is Australian. Believe me Mr Foreman, you would be far more likely to provoke anti-social behaviour from me were you to serve me a single glass of Australian wine than if I were to drink a whole bottle of decent wine. Consequently I will be bringing my own.

I must however thank you for inadvertently giving me an idea. You are probably not aware of my earlier correspondence with Qantas, in which I expressed my fear that whilst we are in Australia our baby might be eaten by a dingo. It has now occurred to me that I can make our baby dingo-proof, as it were, by getting him to drink some Australian wine, thus making him much less palatable. I have tested out this theory on our Labrador, mixing some Shiraz in with his Pal, with the result that he wouldn't go anywhere near it, so if dingoes are anything like our Labrador a dingo wouldn't touch our baby with a bargepole once I've got a bottle of Australian red inside him. I don't suppose there are any laws in Australia governing the amount of wine a baby is allowed to consume, are there?

Yours sincerely

T Ravenscroft (Mr)

The Elms
Wenter Road
New Mills
High Peak
Derbyshire

Air India
17/18 New Bond Street   6th April
LONDON
W1Y 0BD

Dear Air India

I shall be travelling to Bombay with your airline this summer for a holiday, and whilst I am there I hope to buy an elephant. Could you please let me know how much it will cost to fly it back to England? I am afraid that I can't at this stage give you the weight of the elephant, since it depends upon what I can get hold of at the time, but it will have to be a fairly big one as I intend to use it on my smallholding instead of a tractor. (A smallholding is a small English farm in case you're wondering.)

So perhaps you can give me the price of flying a range of elephants, weighing from say 1000 kilograms to 3000 kilograms? But perhaps the exact weight of the elephant isn't important? Maybe you charge by the elephant rather than by the kilo, in which case there won't be a problem.

Looking forward to hearing from you.

Yours faithfully

T Ravenscroft (Mr)

LON/RES/LW/PAX-R/170

APRIL 13

Mr T Ravenscroft
The Elms
Wenter Road
New Mills
High Peak
Derbyshire

Dear Mr Ravenscroft

This has reference to your letter of 06th April.

As the County of Derbyshire is under the jurisdiction of our Manchester Office, we are, by means of a copy of this letter forwarding your letter to them for their action.

In conclusion we would mention that we think it advisable that you contact the Department of Agriculture and Fisheries who will be in a position to inform you as to whether an elephant may be used in the manner in which you intend.

Yours Sincerely

Linda Woolnough
Reservations Superintendent

REGD. OFFICE: AIR INDIA LTD.
HANSALAYA BLDG. 5th FLOOR
15, BARAKHAMBA ROAD
NEW DELHI 110001

17/18 NEW BOND STREET, LONDON W1Y 0BD • CABLES AIRINDIA
PHONE: 081-745 1000 • FAX: 081-745 1019 • TELEX: 934393 AI LHR G

The Elms
Wenter Road
New Mills
High Peak
Derbyshire

Linda Woolnough
Reservations Superintendent   17th April
Air India
17/18 New Bond Street
LONDON
W1Y 0BD

Dear Linda Woolnough

Thank you for your letter of 13th April.

Thank you also for your concern as to whether or not I would be within the law using an elephant on my smallholding. However, you have no need to worry on that score, as I have already cleared the matter with the Department of Agriculture and Fisheries. Incidentally, they think that it is a first-class ecological idea, and have asked me to get in touch with them once I actually have the elephant 'in situ' as it were, as they want to send a man along to conduct an experiment – something to do with feeding the elephant in such a way that its digestive system is working to the optimum, so that when it is pulling the plough it not only cultivates the earth but manures it at the same time. I must say I hadn't thought of that one!

I haven't yet heard from your Manchester office, but in the meantime I wonder if you could help me with a small problem? You see being English and brought up in the city I have no experience of handling elephants, and with this in mind I was wondering whether, during my stay in India, it would be possible for me to have elephant riding lessons? I realise of course that I could walk behind the elephant, as farmers once walked behind their horses, but quite frankly I don't really fancy doing that in view of what I wrote about the elephant manuring the earth. No, I want to learn to ride an elephant like Sabu used to ride one, sat on its head with my legs dangling down either side – although I think I'll skip the loincloth and turban.

Perhaps you could let me have the name of a reputable elephant riding school in the Bombay area? I would be most grateful if you could.

Looking forward to hearing from you.

Yours sincerely

T Ravenscroft (Mr)

The Elms
Wenter Road
New Mills
High Peak
Derbyshire

Iberia International Airways
Ventura House   7th April
27-29 Glasshouse Street
LONDON
W1R 5RG

Dear Iberia International Airways

Returning from Majorca recently on one of your aeroplanes I
purchased from your drinks trolley a 25cl bottle of red Rioja. I
couldn't drink it! I suspected that this might be the case even
before I bought it, as Spanish wines are a long way from being
my favourite product of the grape, so I have no cause for
complaint really, and indeed have no intention of
complaining. I do feel that you are letting yourself down
though, as apart from the wines you offer to your passengers
Iberia run a first-class airline. Could I suggest that instead of
carrying exclusively Spanish wines that you carry at least one
other wine from some other country? Not Australia though,
their wines are as vile as Spanish wines. A decent French
Bordeaux or Rhone perhaps?

However, to get to the point of my letter – which is that after
I left the wine my wife put the screw cap back on the bottle
and took it home with her to use for cooking. There it was put
in a cupboard in the kitchen and promptly forgotten about. A
month later my wife 'found' it, and was going to use it in a
marinade, but unfortunately she knocked it over, some of it
splashing onto our kitchen table, which I had newly
varnished. It took the varnish off the table!

Unfortunately I don't know the name of the bottler of the
wine as my wife threw the bottle in the dustbin, and the
dustmen took it away before I saw what the wine had done to

the table. Therefore I would be very grateful if you could let me know the manufacturer of the wine, as I wish to purchase a quantity.

You might think it odd that I should wish to buy wine which I find undrinkable, and that when opened then left for a month is capable of removing varnish, but the fact is that I am in the furniture renovation business, and in the course of my work have quite often cause to remove varnish from articles of furniture. The stuff I use at the moment costs me over ten pounds a bottle for a 25cl bottle, so the Rioja works out much cheaper and is at the very least just as efficient.

I hope to hear from you soon.

Yours faithfully

T Ravenscroft (Mr)

U.K. & EIRE OFFICES: VENTURE HOUSE, 29 GLASSHOUSE STREET, LONDON W1R 5RG

RESERVATIONS TEL: 071 830 0011
ADMINISTRATION TEL: 071 413 1291 FAX: 071 413 1260
MARKETING TEL: 071 413 1299 FAX: 071 415 0512
CUSTOMER SERVICES TEL: 071 413 1289 FAX: 071 413 1269
LONDON AGENCY SALES TEL: 071 413 1296/6 FAX: 071 413 1261

IBERIA

Reply to UK & Eire Offices
Our ref LONLR R/CL/F

Mr T Ravenscroft
The Elms
Wenter Road
New Mills
High Peak
Derbyshire

12th April

Dear Mr Ravenscroft

I thank you for your letter dated 7th April, and
note that although the red wine offered to our
customers was not to your palate, it has
subsequently, after considerable oxidisation,
proved to be useful as a varnish stripper!

Whilst I have no qualifications whatsoever as a
chemist, I feel sure that it was this long period
of oxidisation which brought about a chemical
reaction so that the resulting liquid could no
longer fit the description of "wine".

However, I do feel qualified to reject the theory
that wines may be classed as good or bad depending
upon the country of their origin! Be assured, Mr
Ravenscroft, that in my considerable experience in
this field there are good and bad wines produced
by all the wine-producing countries!

As it happens, to my taste the wines offered on
board our services vary from "quite acceptable"

BIRMINGHAM
1ST FLOOR
THE MCLAREN BUILDING
MARIS HOUSE CIRCUS
35 DALE END
BIRMINGHAM B4 7LN

RESERVATIONS: 021 643 1953
SALES: 021 212 2205
FAX: 021 212 2712

DUBLIN
54 DAWSON STREET
DUBLIN 2
RESERVATIONS: 010 353 1 779 646
FAX: 010 353 1 793 705

GLASGOW
RESERVATIONS: 041 248 6581

HEATHROW AIRPORT
ROOM 2070, TERMINAL 2
HEATHROW AIRPORT TW6 1JH

TEL: 061 897 7941
FAX: 081 564 9045

LONDON TICKET OFFICE
11-12 HAYMARKET
LONDON SW1Y 4BP

TEL: 071 830 0011
FAX: 071 413 1262

MANCHESTER
IBERIA GROUP
ROOM 1, LEVEL 7
TERMINAL 1 INTERCONTINENTAL
MANCHESTER AIRPORT
MANCHESTER M90 1QX

RESERVATIONS: 061 436 4444
SALES: 061 489 0306
FAX: 061 426 1587

CARGO
BUILDING 562
SHOREHAM ROAD
WORLD CARGO CENTRE
HOUNSLOW
MIDDLESEX TW6 1FV

SALES: 081 897 1476
FAX: 081 564 8575

IBERIA LINEAS AEREAS DE ESPANA S.A. A LIMITED COMPANY INCORPORATED IN SPAIN.

to "excellent", but even individual wines may vary
from one bottle to another, or indeed, the state
of one's palate or indeed stomach at the time.

Nevertheless, in answer to your request for
information, if you were travelling by Viva Air
from Palma directly to London Heathrow, the red
wine will have been Siglo Vino de Crianza,
produces by Bodegas AGE in Fuenmayor, Rioja.

If, on the other hand, you were flying to
Manchester via Barcelona, it may have been one of
five different types of red wine that we carry on
Iberia Airlines services. I enclose the page from
our in-flight magazine with illustrations of the
various bottles which may help you identify the
particular brand.

I hope that this information will prove to be of use
to you. I thank you for your interest, and hope that
we may have the pleasure, and privilege of welcoming
you and Mrs Ravenscroft aboard again soon.

Yours sincerely

THE IBERIA GROUP
Colin Burton
Customer Services Manager

The Elms
Wenter Road
New Mills
High Peak
Derbyshire

Colin Burton
Customer Services Manager   17th April
Iberia International Airways
Ventura House
27-29 Glasshouse Street
LONDON
W1R 5RG

Dear Mr Burton

Thank you for your letter of 12th April.

I have no wish to argue the toss with you about the drinkability or otherwise of Spanish wines, but I do feel I must take you to task regarding your claim that there are good wines and bad wines produced by all the wine-making countries. If we take the definition 'good' to mean 'fresh, well-balanced, pleasant to drink, with no noticeable nasties' – not too difficult a qualification to satisfy I'm sure you will agree – then the next 'good' bottle of Spanish wine I have will be the first. And as for the wine-producing countries of Bulgaria and Romania producing good wines, anyone who believes this is quite frankly living in cloud cuckoo land.

People's perception of wine is completely subjective, so whereas your opinion that the wines offered by Iberia vary from 'quite acceptable' to 'excellent', in my opinion they vary from 'quite horrible' to 'excruciating', so we must agree to differ.

But to the matter of oxidisation, which you put forward as an excuse for the wine's eccentric behaviour. Believe me Mr Burton, the wine was not oxidised, and I know enough about wine, and chemistry, to be able to state this quite categorically.

To confirm my beliefs I had it analysed by an industrial chemist friend of mine, and he concurred. In fact the wine is still not oxidised. The reason that it didn't oxidise after being opened a month ago, is that before my wife put the bottle away she prudently topped it up with wine from a bag-in-box home-made blackberry and elderberry wine – which could only have improved it – then re-sealed it. Therefore the wine's contact with the air was negligible, about two minutes on the aeroplane and about the same at home.

I have recognised the wine in question from the page of your in-flight magazine, which you kindly took the trouble to send, and it is the one on the second row, second from the left. Unfortunately the writing on the label is too small for me to be able to decipher the name of the manufacturer/bottler, so I would be grateful if you could let me have this, and an address where I might obtain supplies of this remarkable product of yours.

Yours sincerely

T Ravenscroft (Mr)

END OF CORRESPONDENCE

The Elms
Wenter Road
New Mills
High Peak
Derbyshire

Sabena Belgian World Airlines
Gemini House   2nd May
2nd Floor
West Block
10-18 Putney Hill
LONDON
SW15 6AA

Dear Sabena Belgian World Airlines

I will be flying to Brussels with your airline in a few weeks'
time, and wonder if I might ask a little favour of you?

The thing is, I'm in the process of building up a new company,
'Rubbers Unlimited', and naturally I'm very anxious to create
the maximum amount of interest in my company's products.
With this in mind, would it be possible for me to attach a two
hundred feet long by forty feet wide banner, in the
approximate shape of a condom, and bearing the legend
'Rubbers Unlimited', to the back of the aeroplane in which I
travel, so that as it wings its way to Brussels following take-off
the whole of London will see it?

I have already had an excellent response from a trial flight
made over Gloucester with a smaller banner attached to a
smaller aeroplane. That was some twelve months ago, and
since then sales in Gloucester have gone up by 32 per cent,
while teenage pregnancies have fallen by 18 per cent; so as
well as helping me you will be doing your bit to bring down
the total of unwanted babies.

Naturally I expect an even greater success with a two hundred
feet wide banner attached to a phallic-shaped jet airliner,
which I suspect might attract quite a lot of attention.

I would be willing to pay Sabena £200 for the privilege of doing this, or you could take three hundred pounds worth of my company's products, whichever you prefer. I recommend the ribbed ones for extra stimulation.

Of course the ideal advertisement for my products would be to encase the entire aeroplane in see-through rubber, with the words 'Rubbers Unlimited' written on the fuselage in giant letters, but at the moment the expense of doing this is a little beyond my advertising budget. One for the future perhaps.

I do hope you will be able to help me on this one.

Yours sincerely

T Ravenscroft (Mr)

The Elms
Wenter Road
New Mills
High Peak
Derbyshire

Air China
41 Grosvenor Gardens   8th April
LONDON
SW1 0BP

Dear Air China

I will be travelling to Beijing in July and would like to take the opportunity of flying with a Chinese airline. However, before I commit myself, I would like to clear up something with regard to the meals you serve up during the flight. Do you serve Chinese food? I mean Chinese food in the sense that 44 Sweet and Sour Chicken and 58 Sliced Beef in Black Bean Sauce is Chinese food? As opposed to food that is bought in China and turned into, for example, Roast Beef and Yorkshire Pudding.

The reason I am asking is that I know you Chinese people could never be accused of being stingy with the monosodium glutamate when it comes to your cookery. Don't get me wrong, I have nothing against MSG, in fact if I owned an MSG factory I would be a very happy man; especially if it happened to be in China, where the natives apparently can't get enough of it. However, the fact is that I am allergic to the stuff. With this in mind, if I were to travel with your airline, would it be possible for me to have an MSG-free meal, or is it all made together in a big pot? If this isn't possible, would it perhaps be in order for me to bring my own food, or would that cause your cabin crew to lose face?

Looking forward to hearing from you

Yours sincerely

T Ravenscroft (Mr)

TOWN OFFICE

41 Grosvenor Gardens
London SW1W 0BP
Tel: 071-6300919/7678
Fax: 071-6307792
Tlx: 9413721 CAAC U. K.
Sita: LONRRCA

AIRPORT OFFICE

RM. 140 Longbridge House
North terminal
Gatwick Airport
West Sussex RH6 ONT
Tel: 0293-502021
Fax: 0293-587525
Tlx: 878856 CAAC U. K.
Sita: LGWAPCA

Mr T Ravenscroft
The Elms
Wenter Road
New Mills
High Peak
Derbyshire

26 April

Dear Mr Ravenscroft

Thank you for your recent query regarding Air China catering.
We are pleased to be able to put your mind at rest – Western
food is served aboard our flights, thus MSG content is minimal.
Should you have special dietary requirements, however, we
would be pleased to pass your request on to our Catering staff
- fortunately the ' big pot' syndrome doesn't apply! If you are
travelling back from Beijing with Air China also, then the same
request must be made locally. Although, again, special needs
should be catered for, it is unusual, as you point out, for Chinese
food to be prepared without MSG, so should you feel more
comfortable supplementing your in-flight food with provisions
of your own, we would assure you that no offence will be taken.

I hope that the above information answers your enquiry,
however should you have any further queries, please do not
hesitate to contact us.

Yours sincerely

Claire Jarrold, Public Relations/Administration Manager
AIR CHINA U.K.

The Elms
Wenter Road
New Mills
High Peak
Derbyshire

Claire Jarrold
Air China   3rd May
41 Grosvenor Gardens
LONDON
SW1 0BP

Dear Claire Jarrold

Thank you for your letter of 26th April.

I am more than a little concerned with your statement that
'Western food is served aboard our flights, thus MSG content is
minimal'. I must stress most forcefully that I cannot eat food
with even the very slightest MSG content, so if there is any
chance whatsoever of MSG being in your food then I am afraid
that it is not for me. Perhaps a meal of fruit, salad, and MSG-free
bread could be made available for me? Would that be possible?

Incidentally, I must congratulate you on your excellent English.
In my business I sometimes have to correspond with Orientals
and I can quite honestly say that your command of written
English is vastly superior to that of most of your fellow Chinese
people. Indeed it is a pleasure to receive a letter that I don't have
to take down to my local Chinese fish-and-chip shop to have
interpreted.

I note also that you have changed your name from Luan Wong
or whatever it was to an English name. Well all I can say is
that if you look half as English as you sound you'll pass for
white any day of the week – although there is nothing to be

ashamed of being Chinese I'm sure – in fact I've always considered the Chinese to be the most generous and courteous people, the Triads gangsters apart of course.

Looking forward to hearing from you.

Yours sincerely

T Ravenscroft (Mr)

AIR CHINA
中国国际航空公司

TOWN OFFICE

41 Grosvenor Gardens
London SW1W OBP
Tel: 071-6300919/7678
Fax: 071-6307792
Tlx: 9413721 CAAC U. K.
Sita: LONRRCA

AIRPORT OFFICE

RM. 140 Longbridge House
North terminal
Gatwick Airport
West Sussex RH6 ONT
Tel: 0293-502021
Fax: 0293-567525
Tlx: 878888 CAAC U. K.
Sita: LGWAPCA

Mr T Ravenscroft
The Elms
Wenter Road
New Mills
High Peak
Derbyshire

12 May

Dear Mr Ravenscroft

Re- MSG-Free Meal

Further to your letter of 03 May, I can confirm that, since you are
unable to tolerate any level of MSG in your food, we would be
pleased to arrange for an MSG-free meal to be provided. Once
your seat has been confirmed and your ticket issued, you may
like to contact us again to give us a more detailed idea of what
you can and can't eat (preferably a week or two before departure).
I would stress again, however, that you may like to arrange
some 'back up' supplies for your Beijing/London journey, in
case your request proves more difficult in China. I hope that this
clarifies the issue for you. We look forward to hearing from you
again at a later date.

Yours sincerely

Claire Jarrold, Public Relations/Administration Manager
AIR CHINA U.K.

The Elms
Wenter Road
New Mills
High Peak
Derbyshire

Claire Jarrold
Air China   18th May
41 Grosvenor Gardens
LONDON
SW1 0BP

Dear Claire Jarrold

Thank you for your letter of 12th May.

I will be booking the flight next week and will let you know the details as soon as I have them. In the meantime here is a list of food that I can and can't eat.

CAN EAT – 3 7 17 18 21 22 32 43 44 49 53 61 77 83 84 110 111 114.

CAN'T EAT – 1 to 120 with the exception of those items listed under CAN EAT.

WON'T EAT – Dog.

Please let me know if this poses any problems.

Yours sincerely

T Ravenscroft (Mr)

The Elms
Wenter Road
New Mills
High Peak
Derbyshire

Varig Brazilian Airlines
16/17 Hanover Street   17th May
LONDON
W1R 0HJ

Dear Varig Brazilian Airways

I will be travelling with your airline to Brazil in September, and am wondering if I could impose on your good nature a little?

The Australian national airline Qantas recently supplied me with a copy of 'Australia – A Traveller's Guide'. I found this publication, despite a distinct lack of information on dingoes eating babies, to be quite invaluable. As Brazil's national airline, are Varig in a position to furnish me with a similar publication covering Brazil?

I would be particularly interested in any guide which carries information on the Amazon Rainforests. Anything you have on this area would be most welcome, especially data on the indigenous Indian population, as I gather that the Brazilian authorities turn a blind eye to the shooting of these rainforest dwellers. Not of course that I intend shooting an Indian; but if while I am out hunting wild game in the Amazon jungle I accidentally bag an Indian by mistake it is comforting to know that the authorities wouldn't be too tiresome about it. And then again I won't make any secret of the fact that a stuffed Indian's head over my sitting room mantelpiece would make a rather interesting talking point.

I look forward to hearing from you.

Yours sincerely

T Ravenscroft (Mr)

Off the beaten track

VARIG
Brazilian Airlines

We have no further supplies
of Parts 1 and 2 available
(of enclosed brochures.

good sources of information are
"The South American Handbook"
cost approx £20.
& "Rough Guide to Brazil"
cost approx £8.

END OF CORRESPONDENCE

The Elms
Wenter Road
New Mills
High Peak
Derbyshire

Malaysia Airlines
61 Piccadilly   13th April
LONDON
W1V 9HL

Dear Malaysia Airlines

I will be travelling to Bangkok with your airline in a few weeks, and I must confess that I'm not looking forward to the experience one little bit! (Going to Bangkok, that is, not flying with your airline – in fact if the stewardesses on Malaysian Airlines aeroplanes are as pretty as I've been led to believe it should be quite pleasant, especially if they wear those skirts with a split up the side.) The thing is, I'm in the cornflour business, and I'll be visiting Thailand in the hope of opening up a new market for my product. The problem is that I will be bringing one-pound samples of cornflour with me, and cornflour looks very much like a certain substance that shall remain nameless, but in which the Thai Government is very down on. (And quite rightly.)

To put it in a nutshell there is no way that I am going to get through the Thai Customs without my little packages of cornflour being given a thorough going over by the local customs officers, with the result that they will almost certainly be in no fit state to make any sort of favourable impression on potential clients. Is there any way of avoiding this upset?

I look forward to hearing from you.

Yours sincerely

T Ravenscroft (Mr)

Malaysia Airlines

61, Piccadilly, London WIV 9HL
191A, Askew Road, London W12 9AX

Askew Road/Piccadilly	:	081 862 0770	Airport Check in	:	081 745 6018
Reservations	:	081 862 0800	Heathrow Traffic	:	081 897 6655
Telex - Askew Road	:	914029 Layang	Heathrow Enquiries	:	081 759 0605
Piccadilly	:	920791 Layang			
Fax – Admin Dept	:	081 862 0117			
Reservations	:	081 740 0159			
Piccadilly	:	071 499 2976			

14 April

LON/E1/0189/ADM

Mr T Ravenscroft
The Elms
Wenter Road
New Mills
High Peak
Derbyshire

Dear Mr Ravenscroft

MALAYSIA AIRLINES – LONDON/KUALA
LUMPUR/BANGKOK

I read you amusing letter and noted the contents. If you could
provide me with your full flight details, we will try and see if our
staff in Bangkok will be able to help with the cornflour.

Yours sincerely

MALAYSIA AIRLINES
WONG TEO KHOON
Assistant to Area Manager UK & Ireland

Malaysia Airlines Incorporated in Malaysia with limited liability and registered in England under No. F. 7707

The Elms
Wenter Road
New Mills
High Peak
Derbyshire

Wong Teo Khoon
Malaysia Airlines   22nd April
61 Piccadilly
LONDON
W1V 9HL

Dear Wong Teo Khoon

Thank you for your letter of 14th April.

I will provide you with the full flight details as soon as I've made the booking, although to tell you the truth I am beginning to have reservations about travelling with an airline whose staff find it amusing that a businessman might have his bags of cornflour gone through, and in all probability ruined. The humour in this situation eludes me completely. Perhaps the word 'cornflour' means something different in the Bahasa Malaysia language? Possibly 'condoms' or something like that, in which case I suppose my letter would provoke some laughter. So I would be grateful therefore if you could point out to me just what is so funny? Or maybe you are being facetious, in which case a letter to your Chairman might not be amiss.

Yours sincerely

T Ravenscroft (Mr)

Malaysia Airlines

61, Piccadilly, London WIV 9HL
191A, Askew Road, London W12 9AX

Askew Road/Piccadilly	: 081 862 0770	Airport Check in	: 081 745 6018
Reservations	: 081 862 0800	Heathrow Traffic	: 081 897 6655
Telex – Askew Road	: 914029 Layang	Heathrow Enquiries	: 081 759 0605
Piccadilly	: 920791 Layang		
Fax – Admin Dept	: 081 862 0117		
Reservations	: 081 740 0159		
Piccadilly	: 071 499 2976		

29 April
LON/PRO/0065/WTK

Mr T Ravenscroft
The Elms
Wenter Road
New Mills
High Peak
Derbyshire

Dear Mr Ravenscroft

MALAYSIA AIRLINES – LONDON/KUALA
LUMPUR/BANGKOK

I am shock to note that you have misinterpret my letter to say that I am being facetious.

My letter is not a joke but to see that I am trying to help you to clear the samples of cornflour at Bangkok Airport. This can only be done by getting our airport staff to meet you on arrival at Bangkok Airport and clear you through the Immigration and Customs. That was my intentions.

Hope you understand my intention.
Yours sincerely

MALAYSIA AIRLINES
WONG TEO KHOON
Assistant to Area Manager UK & Ireland

The Elms
Wenter Road
New Mills
High Peak
Derbyshire

Wong Teo Khoon
Malaysia Airlines   5th May
61 Piccadilly
LONDON
W1V 9HL

Dear Wong Teo Khoon

That better. That more likee it! Not now needing to report you
to Chairman. When arriving me at Bangkok Airport with
sample of cornflour will be sure of telling you before it. Happy
birthday.

Yours sincerely

T Ravenscroft (Mr)

The Elms
Wenter Road
New Mills
High Peak
Derbyshire

Crystal Park 4
2345 Crystal Drive   17th April
Arlington
Virginia
22227
USA

Dear USAir Incorporated

I am currently in the process of setting up a Passenger Aircraft
Museum, and am wondering if you could help me to achieve
this?

I have managed to obtain most of the items which I feel will
be of interest to visitors to my museum, but I am still falling
short of my requirements in the matter of stewardesses'
uniforms. I need five in all, and thus far I have the uniforms
of British Airways, Air China, and South African Airways. A
United States of America uniform, along with the Australian
uniform I expect to be arriving soon from Qantas, would mean
that I would have five stewardesses' uniforms, one from each
of the five continents.

The 'models' on which the stewardess uniforms will be
displayed are a British size 12 – I'm afraid I don't know the
equivalent size on your side of the pond, but I feel sure one of
your lovely stewardesses will know.

I would be quite happy to pay for the uniform, although I
must point out that the other airlines let me have them free of
charge, and I am sure you won't want to be the odd one out.
It doesn't matter if the uniform has been worn, in fact I would
prefer it, as in the interests of authenticity I intend to spray
the uniforms liberally with perfume, so that they will have the

'scent of an airline stewardess', and obviously if the uniform has been worn by one of your stewardesses it will already have this bewitching scent.

Incidentally, you may be able to help me on another matter. The two 'pieces de resistance' of my museum will be a wheel which fell off a Boeing 747 during its descent into Manchester Airport, and a stainless steel aeroplane lavatory which was once sat on by President Nixon – though this was before he became President and disgraced himself, but no less authentic for all that. I am toying with the idea of having a wax effigy of President Nixon sat on the lavatory, but my wife feels that this might be in bad taste. What do you think?

Looking forward very much to receiving the uniform. Have a nice day.

Yours sincerely

T Ravenscroft (Mr)

The Elms
Wenter Road
New Mills
High Peak
Derbyshire

Balkan Bulgarian Airlines
322 Regent Street   22nd April
LONDON
Q1R 5AB

Dear Balkan Bulgarian Airlines

I will shortly be travelling with your airline to Bulgaria for a holiday, accompanied by my wife and my mother-in-law. We will be staying in the Bulgarian Mountains, and I was wondering what the position would be if my mother-in-law slipped and fell down a mountain and met her demise? In this event I am fairly sure that my wife would want to bring the old bag back to England for burial, so I need to know how you stand in Bulgaria with regard to people popping their clogs whilst they are over there. I am aware that in the Mediterranean countries it is the policy to get stiffs planted as soon as possible, and that if we were holidaying in the Med we would have to interrupt our holiday to fly her home, but maybe in Bulgaria, where it isn't quite as hot, you don't mind corpses lying around for a few days, in which case we could finish our holiday before taking her back home with us.

Incidentally, how is a person in a coffin classified on an aeroplane? Do they come under passengers or luggage? And is there any extra charge? If so, it occurs to me that there would be a vacant seat on the return flight – my mother-in-law's – and it seems sensible to me to put the coffin on the seat; in which case I wouldn't expect there to be any charge, especially as she wouldn't be taking any in-flight meals.

Looking forward to hearing from you.

Yours faithfully

T Ravenscroft (Mr)

The Elms
Wenter Road
New Mills
High Peak
Derbyshire

Balkan Bulgarian Airlines
322 Regent Street
LONDON
Q1R 5AB

10th May

Dear Balkan Bulgarian Airlines

I would appreciate a reply to my letter of 22nd April, as I need to know how much money I need to take with me to Bulgaria.

Looking forward to hearing from you.

Yours faithfully

T Ravenscroft (Mr)

16 May

Mr T Ravenscroft
The Elms
Wenter Road
New Mills
High Peak
Derbyshire

Dear Mr Ravenscroft

We received your letter dated 22nd April, In regards to your Mother-in-laws holiday to the mountains in Bulgaria. We did not reply to your letter, as we find it very hard to take serious what you have written.

The only advice we can give to you is, if you are so worried that whilst walking in the mountains with your Mother-in-law, she may fall and meet her demise, then don't take her anywhere near the mountains. Unfortunately we Bulgarians also have the same policy as the Mediterranean Countries, We do like to have our stiffs planted as soon as possible for the obvious reasons.

The summary concludes Mr Ravenscroft to avoid all disaster why not re-think before taking your Mother-in-law on holiday with you.

Yours faithfully

Balkan/Bulgarian Airlines

322 REGENT STREET, LONDON, W1R 5AB
TEL: 071-637 7637/8. ADMIN: 071-631 1263. FAX: 071-637 2481. SITA CODE: LONTOLZ. TELEX: 296547 (BALKAN)

The Elms
Wenter Road
New Mills
High Peak
Derbyshire

Secretary
Balkan Bulgarian Airlines   18th May
322 Regent Street
LONDON
Q1R 5AB

Dear Secretary

Thank you for your letter of 16th May.

Believe me Secretary if I could get out of taking my mother-in-law to the Bulgarian Mountains I would, but not only does the old trout insist on accompanying my wife and I, she is also adamant that she wishes to climb mountains whilst there; and as she is aged eighty-two and has a club foot, it struck me that she may very well come down one of them a lot quicker than she went up, hence my letter to you.

For the life of me I cannot see why you find it hard to take my letter seriously. Perhaps Bulgarians find death amusing? I assure you that I most certainly do not.

I would have thought that an airline would have shown a bit more courtesy to someone who is paying good money to buy airline tickets from them – money, incidentally, which helps to keep people like you in a job – and therefore I would appreciate a reply to my query about bringing occupied coffins back to the UK, and without any further evasions, please.

Yours faithfully

T Ravenscroft (Mr)

BULGARIAN
AIRLINES

24 May

Mr T Ravenscroft
The Elms
Wenter Road
New Mills
High Peak
Derbyshire

Dear Mr Ravenscroft

We would like to apologise for any misunderstanding in the letter dated 16th May.

Balkan Bulgarian Airlines procedures for carrying occupied coffins, would be on the same flight but in the haul section as freight. We do advise you Mr Ravenscroft to take out a holiday insurance before you travel, and this would cover all further expenses for the transportation, if required.

I do hope all your queries have been answered if you have any further questions please do not hesitate to contact us.

Yours faithfully

Balkan Airlines
Admin Secretary

322 REGENT STREET, LONDON, W1R 5AB
TEL: 071-637 7637/8. ADMIN: 071-631 1263. FAX: 071-637 2481. SITA CODE: LONTOLZ. TELEX: 296547 (BALKAN)

The Elms
Wenter Road
New Mills
High Peak
Derbyshire

Admin Secretary
Balkan Bulgarian Airlines   26th May
322 Regent Street
LONDON
Q1R 5AB

Dear Admin Secretary

Thank you for your letter of 24th May and the advice about taking out holiday insurance to cover the cost of bringing the coffin back to the UK.

Unfortunately all the travel insurance companies refuse to insure my mother-in-law following an accident the last time we took her on holiday when she tried to break one of the aeroplane windows with a machete, with the result that we had to turn back. I would therefore like you to advise me what any further costs for coffin transportation would amount to, if that isn't too much trouble?

Yours faithfully

T Ravenscroft (Mr)

The Elms
Wenter Road
New Mills
High Peak
Derbyshire

Air Zimbabwe Corporation
Colette House   16th April
52-55 Piccadilly
LONDON
W1V 9AA

Dear Air Zimbabwe

It has long been an ambition of mine to visit South Africa, but unfortunately my principles have never allowed me to come to terms with the policy of apartheid.

However, now that the South African Government has at last come to its senses, I am able to achieve my ambition. But first I need to satisfy myself that apartheid, as applied to air travel, has been outlawed in deed as well as in word. The reason I feel this may not always be the case is because of something I read recently in a magazine article. The writer made the point that when apartheid was the order of the day whites sat at the front of the aeroplane and blacks sat at the rear, and now that apartheid has been shelved all airlines flying in South African airspace have been instructed to abandon this system of segregation.

Unfortunately it would appear that some of the airlines in question have failed to enter into the spirit of things, and whilst abandoning the policy of seating the whites at the front of the aeroplane and the blacks at the rear, have replaced it with a policy of seating the whites on the right side of the aeroplane and the blacks on the left – and in one case the whites on the inside of the aeroplane and the blacks on the outside of the aeroplane.

Needless to say my feelings on the subject of segregation would not allow me to travel with an airline which adopted such a policy, and before I book a flight with your airline I would like you to confirm that you do not adopt a policy of segregation in any way, shape or form. I look forward to hearing from you to this effect.

Incidentally, I don't object to segregation by first class, club class and economy class. To the contrary, I find the idea of a South African First Class black most refreshing.

Yours faithfully

T Ravenscroft (Mr)

Air Zimbabwe Corporation
Colette House, 52-55 Piccadilly
London W1V 9AA
Tel.: Reservations 071 - 491 - 0009
Admin: 071 - 499 - 8947
Fax: 071 - 355 3326
Telex: 25251 AIRZIM G
SITA: LONSSUM

air zimbabwe

Member Of

21st April

Mr T Ravenscroft
The Elms
Wenter Road
New Mills
High Peak
Derbyshire

Dear Sir

RE: VISIT TO SOUTH AFRICA

I acknowledge reciept of your letter dated 16TH April,
with thanks and have pleasure of advising you that
air Zimbabwe does not practise any racial segregation as
an IATA carrier.

At the time any passenger books with our carrier, the
passenger is free to chose where he/she prefers to sit eg
window seat, isle, smoking or non smoking seats in the
booking class of his/her fare.

I have enclosed a seating plan in case you wish to reserve
your seat as you make your reservations/

Air Zimbabwe look forward to welcoming you on board.

Yours sincerely

T.H. MUKUSHA
REGIONAL MANAGER UK AND IRELAND

FOR OFFICE USE	DATE
FIRST ACTION	
FINAL ACTION	

FLY THE NATIONAL AIRLINE
AIR ZIMBABWE

APPLICATION FORM FOR EMPLOYMENT

Use Block Letters Please

1. Post applied for .... or ....

2. Surname .... Initial(s) ....

3. Age .... Date of Birth ....

4. Residential Address .... Tel. No. ....

   ....

   b Business Address .... Tel. No. ....

   ....

5. Citizenship .... Passport No. ....

6. If you have children give details of age and sex ....

   ....

   ....

7. Please indicate by an X your highest level of academic achievement:

Grade 7 Std. 6	ZJC Grade 9	ZCE NCE	O' Level Grade II	M Level	A Level
19	19	19	19	19	19 ....

The Elms
Wenter Road
New Mills
High Peak
Derbyshire

T H Mukusha
Air Zimbabwe Corporation
Colette House
52-55 Piccadilly
LONDON
W1V 9AA

24th April

Dear T H Mukusha

Thank you for your letter of 21st April.

Something must have gone wrong at your end because you did not include a seating plan as stated but an application form for employment at Air Zimbabwe.

I have studied this form closely and nowhere in it does it try to find out if the applicant is black or white – unless the educational qualification ZCE means Zulu Certificate of Education, but I wouldn't know this – so your claim that you do not practise racial segregation would appear to hold water.

However, the mistake you made does give me more than a little cause for concern with regard to the advisability of flying with your airline – if Air Zimbabwe can't do a simple thing like enclosing the correct form in an envelope how can I be sure that your pilot won't fly me to South America instead of South Africa?

If you can manage to send me another letter, this time enclosing the seating plan, my fears might go away.

Yours sincerely

T Ravenscroft (Mr)

The Elms
Wenter Road
New Mills
High Peak
Derbyshire

TAP Air Portugal
Gillingham House   18th April
38/44 Gillingham Street
LONDON
SW1 V1HU

Dear TAP Air Portugal

On a recent TAP Air Portugal flight to Madeira I overheard the
following comment, made by a fat lady who was seated across
the central aisle from me. She said, as near as I can remember,
'You can bet your life that if I'm sat on the right-hand side of
the aeroplane the Captain will say: "If passengers on the left-
hand side of the aeroplane look through the window they will
be able to see such-and-such a place." And if I'm sat on the
left-hand side he will say: "If passengers sitting on the right-
hand side look through the window they will be able to see
such-and-such a place." Whatever the Captain announces I'm
always on the wrong side of the aeroplane, I never get to see
anything, and it really pisses me off.'

About half an hour later the Captain announced over the PA
system that passengers on the left-hand side of the aeroplane
could now see the coastline of the Algarve. Whereupon the
fat lady, who was sitting on the right-hand side, said: 'Oh I've
had enough of this shit!' sprang to her feet, and attempted to
see the coastline of the Algarve through the left-hand
window, adjacent to the row of seats in which I was seated.
Almost immediately the aeroplane must have hit an air
pocket or something, because it suddenly tilted sharply to the
left, with the result that the fat lady lurched forward and fell
on top of me.

Fortunately no damage was done, except to the fat lady's pride – she was wearing a flimsy sun-top and one of her breasts fell out – but the fact remains that if the Captain had refrained from making it known that passengers on the left-hand side could see the coastline of the Algarve the incident would never have happened.

It is my intention to write to the Airline Authorities with the object of getting them to ban announcements by flight crews about geographical features which can be seen from the right-hand/left-hand side of aeroplanes, and in view of the incident reported above I would expect your blessing. Can I therefore have your permission to mention to the authorities that I have your support in this matter?

Yours faithfully

T Ravenscroft (Mr)

AIR PORTUGAL

Unit 10, Haslemere Industrial Estate
Silver Jubilee Way
Cranford. Middlesex TW4 6NG

Our ref. LHRSC/JG
Your ref

Mr T Ravenscroft
The Elms
Wenter Road
New Mills
High Peak
Derbyshire

Dear Mr Ravenscroft

We are in receipt of your letter dated April 18. In order
that we may properly assess your request, we would
very much appreciate you advising us of the flight
number involved and the date.

We need to ascertain how the announcements were
made and if they were within our accepted criteria,
before our Head Office can comment further.

Yours sincerely,

J Greenall
Customer Services

ADMIN/ACCOUNTS/SALES: 01-828 6599 RESERVATIONS: 01-828 0262 Cables: AEROTAP LONDON Telex: 261239
TICKET SALES OFFICE: 01-839 1031 LONDON (HEATHROW) AIRPORT Terminal 2: 01-745 7271
CARGO OFFICE: 01-759 1166 or 01-897 4546 MANCHESTER: 061-499 1161

The Elms
Wenter Road
New Mills
High Peak
Derbyshire

J Greenall
Customer Services
TAP Air Portugal
Unit 10
Silver Jubilee Way
CRANFORD
TW4 6NG

3rd May

Dear J Greenall

Thank you for your undated letter which I received yesterday.

I am more than a little disturbed at your reply. Announcements advising passengers that they can see certain geographical features out of the window are clearly dangerous, especially when obstreperous fat women are on board, yet you are clearly reticent about doing anything which would eliminate the danger.

However, for the record, the flight was from Funchal to London, on the 10th of April, I can't remember the flight number, and the announcement, in English with a very Portuguese accent, went something like: 'If passengers sitting on the left side of our aeroplane are looking out of the window they will be seeing the coastline of our very nice Algarve region.'

I await the comments of your Head Office, but not for too long.

Yours faithfully

T Ravenscroft (Mr)

AIR PORTUGAL

Unit 10, Haslemere Industrial Estate
Silver Jubilee Way
Cranford, Middlesex TW4 6NG

Our ref. LHRSC/JG
Your ref
10 May

Mr T Ravenscroft
The Elms
Wenter Road
New Mills
High Peak
Derbyshire

Dear T Ravenscroft

Further to our previous letter and your response of 03 May, we regret that despite thorough searching, we are unable to trace any record of you having travelled on any TAP Air Portugal flight from London on 10 April to either Funchal, Lisbon or Faro.

Subsequently, we are unable to locate the flight to which you referred. However, with regard to your request, we understand your points regarding announcements, but as we have to strike a balance with passengers wishes, we must also accede to passengers comments that not enough information is given.

It is always recommended that passengers remain seated during a flight, except when using toilet facilities, but we cannot be held responsible for the bad manners and alleged boorish behaviour of certain passengers. If a passenger became a constant nuisance, the crew have the authority to restrain them.

ADMIN/ACCOUNTS/SALES: 01-828 6599 RESERVATIONS: 01-828 0262 Cables: AEROTAP LONDON Telex: 261239
TICKET SALES OFFICE: 01-839 1031 LONDON (HEATHROW) AIRPORT Terminal 2: 01-745 7271
CARGO OFFICE: 01-759 1166 or 01-897 4546 MANCHESTER: 061-499 1161

We very much regret any inconvenience, but would confirm that we have no plans to alter our announcement procedures at the present time. However, your comments are well noted and will be used in future evaluations for in-flight service levels.

Yours sincerely,

J Greenall
Customer Services

The Elms
Wenter Road
New Mills
High Peak
Derbyshire

J Greenall
Customer Services   17th May
TAP Air Portugal
Unit 10
Silver Jubilee Way
CRANFORD
TW4 6NG

Dear J Greenall

Reference your letter dated 10th May.

The reason that you were unable to trace any record of my
having travelled with TAP Air Portugal is because I am a rather
famous writer, 'T Ravenscroft' being my nom-de-plume, and
whenever I travel I always go under my real name. Actually I
am surprised you haven't remarked on the fact and asked me
for a signed photograph, people usually do.

As a writer, could I pass on a little tip to you? Always try to put
the words of a sentence in such an order that they do not lead
to confusion.

For example, in your letter you have written 'It is always
recommended that passengers remain seated during a flight,
except when using toilet facilities.' Anyone reading this could
quite easily interpret it to mean that when using the toilet
facilities they should not remain seated, in other words that
they should stand up – which may be all very well in the case
of a man having a number one, but would be distinctly tricky
for him were he to be having a number two – and would be
equally tricky for a woman having either.

As far as the rest of your letter is concerned I am afraid that we must agree to differ. Bearing in mind your comment that you must also accede to passengers' comments that not enough information is given, I suppose I must be grateful that as well as holding forth with spurious announcements about what can be seen through the windows, your Captain doesn't fill in the intervening time with a few songs – especially if he included 'I See The Moon' in his repertoire when someone was using the toilet standing up!

Yours faithfully

T Ravenscroft (Mr)

END OF CORRESPONDENCE

Turkish Airlines
11/12 Hanover Street
LONDON
W1R 9HF

The Elms
Wenter Road
New Mills
High Peak
Derbyshire

24th April

Dear Turkish Airlines

I will be flying with your airline to Turkey in a couple of months, but before I visit your country I would be grateful if you could help me with a little query.

Geography has never been my strong suit and when I looked up Turkey on the map I was quite alarmed to discover just how near it is to Kurdistan, and I'm sure I've no need to tell you that this is where the Iraqis quite often wage war with the local populace. Personally I think that the Iraqis should let the Kurds have their whey – a little joke there – but that's another matter.

The thing is, Kurdistan is far too close to Turkey for my liking, and just in case Iraq tries to enlarge its little empire at your expense while I'm over there I am considering bringing my shotgun along to protect myself with, should the need arise. Would this be in order? If not, is it possible to buy a decent firearm in Turkey? I am told that the Turks will try to sell anything to tourists – in fact a friend of mine told me he had bought a hooker in a tobacco shop in Bodrum. However I won't be bothering myself because I have never had to pay for sex in my life and I don't intend starting now. But does the Turks' overpowering desire to sell things to tourists extend to firearms?

I look forward to hearing from you.

Yours sincerely

T Ravenscroft (Mr)

The Elms
Wenter Road
New Mills
High Peak
Derbyshire

Alitalia   22nd April
205 Holland Park Road
LONDON
W11 4XB

Dear Alitalia

My recent trip to Rome with your airline was the first I have made for several years, and it came as a great disappointment to discover that the emergency procedures are now given via TV screens and not, as used to be the case, by your air stewardesses.

I can't speak for other men of course, but as a student of human nature I would wager a couple of Pavarotti tickets to a bowl of spaghetti that the vast majority of the male sex would prefer to see the stewardesses doing the emergency drills again. To see one of these lovelies donning a life jacket used to be the high point of the journey. Even seen from several yards away it was never less than an enjoyable experience to see the stewardess stretching her torso this way and that, and pointing at it, but if one happened to be fortunate enough to be seated adjacent to where she was doing it – Mamma Mia!

I would have thought that as Italians, and what that entails – you know, hot blood and all that – that you would have been well aware of what a treat it was for your male passengers to see nubile young women stretching and pointing at their torsos, but apparently not.

However, I'm sure that now I've pointed it out to you that you'll soon put a stop to this nonsense with the TV screens and get your stewardesses back to performing 'live' again.

Incidentally, I will be taking a party of balsamic-vinegar-lovers to Tuscany in August. Do you offer any discounts for parties of twenty?

Yours faithfully

T Ravenscroft (Mr)

Alitalia

205 Holland Park Avenue
London W11 4XB

24th May OM/1571/590
Mr T Ravenscroft
The Elms
Wenter Road
New Mills
High Peak
Derbyshire

Dear Mr Ravenscroft

We thank you for your letter dated 22 April and wish to apologise for the delay in our reply.

Although your humorous comments regarding the 'traditional way' of demonstrating the emergency procedures have been duly noted, we wish to point out that the TV screens have proved to be a great success and are increasingly adopted by a great number of airlines world-wide.

With regard to the group you will be taking to Tuscany in August, may we suggest that you contact our sales department in this connection at the following telephone number ███████████.

We thank you for having brought this matter to our attention and hope that we shall be given an early opportunity to welcome you on board in the near future.

Yours sincerely,

ALITALIA
Linee aeree Italiane SpA
L. Basso
Passenger Marketing Manager

Linee Aeree Italiane S.p.A.
Area Office for the UK & Ireland
Incorporated with limited liability in Italy
Registered in England as a branch
under no. BR1133

The Elms
Wenter Road
New Mills
High Peak
Derbyshire

L Basso
Passenger Marketing Manager   30th May
Alitalia
205 Holland Park Road
LONDON
W11 4XB

Dear L Basso

Thank you for your letter of 24th May, but despite your name I can't really believe that you are a real Italian. All the Italians I know would no more favour a TV emergency procedure over stewardesses doing it in the flesh than they would favour a black pudding over a pizza napolitano.

I have found out that Balkan Bulgarian Airlines still use stewardesses to go through the emergency procedures, so we will be travelling with them, then making our way overland to Tuscany from Sofia. It is a bit of a detour I know, but should be well worth it. There is of course a risk that being Slavonic the stewardesses may have moustaches but that is a risk we are willing to take. It wouldn't surprise me if you lost many more passengers through your attitude on this subject.

Yours faithfully

T Ravenscroft (Mr)

END OF CORRESPONDENCE

The Elms
Wenter Road
New Mills
High Peak
Derbyshire

Czechoslovak Airlines
72 Margaret Street
LONDON
W1N 7HA

23rd April

Dear Czechoslovak Airlines

Flying with your airline on the 12.15 flight from Prague to London Heathrow on the 20th of April, I inadvertently left my false teeth in one of the toilets. I suppose that someone will have handed them in by now, so if you could send them on to me at the above address I would very much appreciate it; registered mail please as the dentures feature two gold teeth and are quite valuable.

I will of course reimburse you with the cost of posting the teeth to me.

Yours faithfully

T Ravenscroft (Mr)

CSA / CZECHOSLOVAK AIRLINES

72 MARGARET STREET, LONDON W1N 7HA

Mr T Ravenscroft
The Elms
Wenter Road
New Mills
High Peak
Derbyshire

06th May

Dear Mr Ravenscroft

Further to your letter of 23rd April regarding
your lost property. We would like to confirm that
you letter has been sent to our lost property
department in Prague who will notify us if your
property is found.

We close in assuring you of our attention in this
matter.

Yours sincerely

Mr J Bebiak
Director UK and Ireland

RESERVATIONS
TEL. 071 255 1898
FAX. 071 323 1633

ADMINISTRATION
TEL. 071 255 1366
TELEX 265776

HEATHROW AIRPORT
TEL. 081 745 7176
FAX. 081 745 7259

Registered U.K. Office: 72 Margaret Street, London W1   No. FCO 14939   Member of I.A.T.A. Incorporated in Czech Republic 45795908 Ruzyne Prahkc

Mr J Bebiak
Czechoslovak Airlines
72 Margaret Street
LONDON
W1N 7HA

9th May

Dear Mr J Bebiak

Since leaving my false teeth on your aeroplane I have once again travelled with your airline from London to Prague and back. As luck would have it several if not all of the cabin staff were the very same people who were on the first flight. During that flight I couldn't help noticing that one of your stewardesses was wearing poor quality false teeth. (People who wear false teeth notice that sort of thing in other false-teeth wearers.)

After taking the more recent flight I can hazard a guess that your lost property department in Prague will not come up with my false teeth. This is because they are now in the mouth of the stewardess who was wearing the poor quality false teeth on the first flight. She must have spotted them in the lavatory, recognised immediately that they were a far superior set compared with her own, and decided to keep them for her own use rather than hand them in.

Unfortunately I have no way of proving this, but if, as I suspect, the teeth fail to turn up in your lost property office then the thing is pretty much cut and dried – since the teeth must be somewhere, and if they are not on your aeroplane or in your lost property office where else could they be but in the mouth of your stewardess?

Yours faithfully

T Ravenscroft (Mr)

CZECHOSLOVAK AIRLINES

72 MARGARET STREET, LONDON W1N 7HA

Mr T Ravenscroft
The Elms
Wenter Road
New Mills
High Peak
Derbyshire
————————

Prague, 9 June
G.B.

Dear Mr Ravenscroft

We confirm receipt of your letter dated April 23rd related your lost while travelling on Czechoslovak Airlines on April 20th.

We are very sorry but we like to inform you that we didn't found your false teeth on the board of this aircraft. You will be advised to inform yourself about your lost at Heathrow Airport – Lost/Found Dpt.

Kindly accept our apology for this unfavourable information and assure you of our attention.

Yours faithfully

JUDr.Jarmila Kocova

END OF CORRESPONDENCE

RESERVATIONS
TEL. 071 255 1898
FAX. 071 323 1633

ADMINISTRATION
TEL. 071 255 1366
TELEX 265776

HEATHROW AIRPORT
TEL. 081 745 7176
FAX. 081 745 7259

Registered U.K. Office: 72 Margaret Street, London W1   No. FCO 14839   Member of I.A.T.A. Incorporated in Czech Republic 45795908 Ruzyne Prahkc

The Elms
Wenter Road
New Mills
High Peak
Derbyshire

Dear LOT Polish Airlines
313 Regent Street
LONDON
W1R 7PE

24th April

Dear LOT Polish Airlines

I have travelled recently with your airline to Warsaw, and having done so I can't help but feel that LOT Polish Airlines is a few slices short of a salami in the 'image' department; your otherwise perfectly good airline being badly let down by the drab livery of your aeroplanes, which does absolutely nothing for them.

I am in the advertising game so I know that image is of paramount importance. You will appreciate that I know my business inside out when I tell you that I was involved in the recent award-winning Boddington's Beer TV commercials.

Another idea of mine is 'Catholic Condoms'. This I feel will go a long way to solving the moral dilemma of Catholics, who are afraid they might catch some sexually transmitted disease, but whose faith won't allow them to use a contraceptive device, and will receive its national TV launch at the end of July with the slogan – 'Catholic Condoms – the ones with a hole in them!'

I have some very positive ideas for re-designing the LOT Polish Airlines aeroplane livery and logo, and as my wife is half Polish I am prepared to do the job for half price. Now I can't be fairer than that, can I?

Would you please let me know by return if you find my proposal of interest?

Yours faithfully

T Ravenscroft (Mr)

PS. How about 'What a LOT I got!' as a slogan for starters?

313 Regent Street
LONDON W1R 7PE
Tel: 071-580 5037
Fax: 071-323 0774
Telex: 27860
SITA Code: LONTOLO

Mr T Ravenscroft
The Elms
Wenter Road
New Mills
High Peak
Derbyshire

Dear Mr Ravenscroft

Thank you for your letter and all the warm words about LOT Polish Airlines.

We would like to inform you that change of the livery of our planes is a very expensive undertaking and it is not planned for the near future.

We would also like to wish you all the best in your new campaign and hope to see you on board our planes again.

Yours sincerely,

K Rutkowska-Parkes

END OF CORRESPONDENCE

The Elms
Wenter Road
New Mills
High Peak
Derbyshire

KLM Royal Dutch Airlines   25th April
Plesman House
190 Great South West Road
FELTHAM
TW15 9RL

Dear KLM Royal Dutch Airlines

I always make a point of travelling with the national airline whenever taking a holiday in a foreign country, as I find that one gets the impression of the holiday actually beginning from the moment one boards the aeroplane; so when I fly to Amsterdam at the end of next month it will be with your airline. I trust that you serve genuine Dutch cuisine during the flight, as I have long been a fan of your famous Edam cheese – although it must be said I wouldn't kill somebody for another chunk of your Gouda. So I hope I won't be disappointed vis-à-vis the food!

Actually, speaking of disappointments, I have already had one before I even arrive in the Netherlands. Talking to a friend who has already visited your country I was saddened to hear from him that you have a lot of dykes over there. Personally I have no time for them, but I suppose that a woman's sexual preferences are entirely her own business when it comes to the rub, and I don't suppose it will spoil my holiday – anyway your tulips and windmills will more than make up for it I am sure. But to the point of my letter; which is that at the time of travelling with you I will have a broken leg. This being the case I was wondering if I might have a little preferential treatment? I believe that airlines allow people who are handicapped in this manner to board and leave the aeroplane first, and provide a privileged seat for them, so I would like a little bit of that if it is all the same to you.

Looking forward to hearing from you.

Yours faithfully

T Ravenscroft (Mr)

KLM

Guidelines for the transport of physically impaired passengers

The material (suggestions)contained herein are not intended nor should be construed as a substitute for individual professional medical advice.

The Elms
Wenter Road
New Mills
High Peak
Derbyshire

KLM Royal Dutch Airlines
Plesman House   2nd May
190 Great South West Road
FELTHAM
TW15 9RL

Dear KLM Royal Dutch Airlines

Thank you for your booklet 'Guidelines for the Transport of Physically Impaired Passengers', which I received today.

May I first of all congratulate you on providing such a comprehensive service for those passengers with special needs. Apparently, were I a passenger who suffered from disorders of the heart, had undergone recent surgery, had a complicated pregnancy, couldn't take care of myself because I was mentally unstable, needed an intravenous drip, couldn't use a normal seat, needed additional leg room, had behavioural problems which required attention by an escort, needed oxygen during the flight, required a low residue diet, and had no control over my bladder and bowel functions, you would still be able to cope with me. Wonderful!

However, my requirements are much simpler. I appear to come somewhere between your WCHR category – 'Passengers whose impairment of walking requires a wheelchair, but who can ascend/descend aircraft steps and make their own way to/from their cabin seat', and your Physically Impaired category – 'who in principle can attend to their own needs during the flight, but who might be helped by some extra attention.' In other words I may need a little help from one of your stewardesses in walking to the toilet. (Not of course that I have no control over my bladder and bowel movements, you understand – all is quite normal in that department thank you very much, and I only envisage one trip to your facilities at the most.)

However, I must insist on one thing. And that is your absolute guarantee that the stewardess who escorts me to the toilet is 100 per cent heterosexual. As I said in my initial letter, if a woman chooses to be a dyke that's her business, it's just that I can't bear the thought of being touched by one of them.

Is KLM Royal Dutch Airlines able to give me this guarantee?

Yours faithfully

T Ravenscroft (Mr)

KLM UK & Ireland

Mr T Ravenscroft
The Elms
Wenter Road
New Mills
High Peak
Derbyshire

18th May

Dear Mr Ravenscroft

Thank you for your letter dated 2nd May.

We note that you are able to ascend/descend aircraft steps and are in a position to attend to your own needs during the flight. The only requirement, therefore, is a wheelchair assistance which we will be quite happy to request for you once you have made a reservation with us.

Every effort Is made by our crew members to make the flight comfortable for all our passengers but as you will understand we are unable to guarantee requests which are uncharacteristic or of rather an unusual nature.

Please ensure you request wheelchair assistance when you call to make your booking.

We now look forward to welcome you on board KLM.

Yours sincerely,

A.J.KANJARIA
SUPERVISOR SPECIAL FACILITIES

KLM Royal Dutch Airlines
Plesman House, 190 Great South West Road, Feltham, Middlesex TW14 9RL.
Telephone: 081 750 9200 Reservations : Telephone: 081 750 9000 Fax: 081 750 9090
Registered Office: Amsterdam, 55 Amsterdamseweg, Holland Registered No. 14266

The Elms
Wenter Road
New Mills
High Peak
Derbyshire

A J Kanjaria
KLM Royal Dutch Airlines
Plesman House
190 Great South West Road
FELTHAM
TW15 9RL

24th May

Dear A J Kanjaria

Thank you for your letter of 18th May.

I am sorry that you are unable to guarantee that the stewardess who helps me to the toilet will be a heterosexual. Consequently I am unable to guarantee that if she is a lesbian and lays so much as a finger on me that she won't end up in far more need of a wheelchair than I am!

Yours sincerely

T Ravenscroft (Mr)

The Elms
Wenter Road
New Mills
High Peak
Derbyshire

Japan Airlines
Hanover Square
5 Hanover Courts
LONDON
W1R 0DR

28th April

Dear Japan Airlines

I am afraid that I have a complaint to make about your airline. On the return trip from Osaka to London recently your cabin staff served me some uncooked fish. When I say uncooked I don't mean that it was merely underdone, or even grossly underdone, I mean fish that wasn't in any way done – in fact I will go as far as to say that the nearest the fish came to having any heat applied to it was when I took the cover off the plate and the sun shone on it through the window. I heard someone refer to it as 'sooshy' or something like that.

I couldn't eat it of course, although, I must admit, I saw several Japanese businessmen tucking into it with apparent relish – but then you Japanese think nothing of committing suicide by throwing yourselves on your swords do you, so you obviously have stronger stomachs than we occidentals.

Oddly enough the rest of the meal was quite exemplary and cooked to perfection, so I think you ought to have a word with whoever cooks your fish and tell him to get his act together before you start losing passengers.

Yours faithfully

T Ravenscroft (Mr)

Japan Airlines
Regional Office United Kingdom & Ireland
Hanover Court
5 Hanover Square
London W1R 0DR
Reservations 071-408 1000
Fax 071-499 1071
Telex 23692
When replying to this letter
please telephone: 071-408

T. Ravenscroft, Esq.,
The Elms
Wenter Road
New Mills
High Peak
Derbyshire

24 May

Dear Sir,

With reference to your letter of 19th May and a previous letter you refer to of 28th April.

We regret to advise you that we have not received your letter of 28th April. However, in order that we may make the necessary enquiries with our Cabin Services Office regarding the menu onboard your flight, we would appreciate your advising the flight number and date of travel. Upon receipt of your reply, we shall contact our Cabin Services Office with a copy of your letter requesting their inquiry into this matter.

Yours faithfully

G.C. McKenzie
Deputy Regional Manager -
Passenger Sales, UK & Ireland
GCM/JA.M

Japan Airlines Company Limited. Incorporated with Limited Liability in Japan
Head Office: Tokyo Bldg, 2-7-3 Marunouchi, Chiyoda-Ku, Tokyo
Registered in England FC004934 BR000826

The Elms
Wenter Road
New Mills
High Peak
Derbyshire

26th May

G.C. McKenzie
Japan Airlines
Hanover Square
5 Hanover Courts
LONDON
W1R 0DR

Dear G.C. McKenzie

Thank you for your letter of 24th May.

My sincerest apologies. Since writing to you I have learned that it is the custom in Japan to eat raw fish. Not only that, it is regarded as a delicacy!

I suppose what you do in Japan is your business, and that if you want to eat raw fish it is entirely your concern and nobody else's, although how anyone in their right mind can prefer a lump of raw fish to a nicely grilled Birds Eye fish finger is quite beyond me.

However, this does not mean that I don't find the idea of you trying to force raw fish on British people goes quite beyond the pale. This is because I have also learned that the eating of raw fish is responsible for many deaths by poison every year.

Consequently I have reported you to the Ministry of Health.

Yours sincerely

T Ravenscroft (Mr)

The Elms
Wenter Road
New Mills
High Peak
Derbyshire

United Airlines
United House
Building 451
Southern Perimeter Road
Heathrow Airport
Middlesex
TW6 3LT

1st May

Dear United Airlines

I wish to travel to Hong Kong later this year and am wondering if I might fly with you?

Since last flying, some years ago, I have become a somnambulist. Naturally enough I don't want to take the risk of sleepwalking whilst I am in an aeroplane – in a somnambulistic state I could quite easily open one of the doors and plunge to my death!

The answer to my problem would seem to be for me to remain awake for the duration of the flight, but unfortunately all forms of transport have the effect of sending me to sleep – five minutes on a train, boat or plane and I am deep in the Land of Nod.

Bearing the above in mind, would it be possible for me to stand up throughout the journey? I realise of course that you have regulations about passengers remaining seated with fastened seat belts during certain times, but in this instance I am hoping you might stretch a point – after all your stewardesses still parade up and down with the duty-free whilst passengers are seated, don't they?

Apart from that I wouldn't be able to sit down even if I wanted to, not with any degree of comfort at least, since I intend to wear a parachute. This is because I have been known to fall asleep even when stood up on transport, and if I do happen to sleepwalk and open one of the doors and fall out of the aeroplane – which would no doubt wake me up – I want to be able to hit terra firma with as soft a landing as possible.

I do hope that you will be able to help me.

Yours faithfully

T Ravenscroft (Mr)

UNITED AIRLINES

United House
Southern Perimeter Road
Heathrow Airport, Middlesex TW6 3LP

May 5
Our ref: Corres.RA.RC.G
Mr. T. Ravenscroft,
The Elms
Wenter Road
New Mills
High Peak
Derbyshire

Dear Mr. Ravenscroft,

Thank you for your letter expressing your desire to fly with United to Hong Kong.

Your unfortunate affliction must make all forms of travel extremely difficult and we can sympathise with your problem. At United we always try to accommodate our customers' special needs but are unable to guarantee that you would remain awake on such a long journey. Safety is our number one priority and we would not wish for you to inadvertantly tamper with the aircraft doors.

Standing for any length of time is regrettably not permitted as we have no hanging straps to hold and it can get bumpy especially when turning and landing. It could endanger both yourself and other passengers.

Thank you for your interest in flying United and we hope your condition will improve to enable you to travel safely in the future.

Yours sincerely

RICHARD CORKER
DUTY MANAGER

The Elms
Wenter Road
New Mills
High Peak
Derbyshire

Richard Corker
United Airlines   9th May
United House
Building 451
Southern Perimeter Road
Heathrow Airport
Middlesex
TW6 3LT

Dear Mr Corker

Thank you for your letter dated 5th May.

United Airlines are the fourth airline I have written to with regard to my travelling problems and the first to honour me with a reply, so yours is obviously a more caring airline than the others. You don't care quite enough to see your way to fly me to Hong Kong, but at least it's a start.

The stumbling block in the way of my travelling with you would seem to be your concern, and rightly so, that I might inadvertently tamper with the aircraft doors. Perhaps I could offer a couple of suggestions, which might enable us to get round this problem?

1. Tie or chain me securely to my seat throughout the duration of the flight, so that it is quite impossible for me to walk around. (So that any passengers sitting nearby wouldn't worry unduly, you could tell them that I was an escaped drug-trafficker or something, who was being returned to Hong Kong for execution.)

2. Allow me to travel in the hold as baggage. I could be put in a suitable container, say a crate, with the top securely screwed down, with holes drilled in it so that I could breathe. Then if one of the United Airlines staff could be on hand to unscrew the crate at the Hong Kong end – and screw me back in again for the return journey – then all would be hunky-dory. Naturally I wouldn't expect to pay as much for being treated as baggage, but as you will be screwing me as well I would be more than happy to pay you what I would pay for a seat.

Either of the above methods would suit me just fine, and I look forward to hearing from you as to which method best suits you lovely people at United Airlines.

Yours sincerely

T Ravenscroft (Mr)

The Elms
Wenter Road
New Mills
High Peak
Derbyshire

1st May

Finnair
14 Clifford Street
LONDON
W1X 1RD

Dear Finnair

I will be making a return visit to Finland with your airline in a few weeks' time, and am wondering if you could let me have some information with regard to your airline?

During my stay in Finland, the purpose of which is to undertake the Finnish section of an independently sponsored study of Northern Europeans, I will be trying to discover why it is that Finnish people are so miserable.

Up until the time I became involved in the study, the only Finns I had ever met were those taking holidays in the Mediterranean, and I'd always assumed that what made them so miserable was the thought of having to go back to Finland at the end of the holiday.

However, when visiting Finland last year, I came into contact with many of the natives who were equally miserable, and despite the fact that they had never been out of the country. So there is obviously more to it than I at first thought.

Quite why the sponsors want to know why Finns are miserable isn't clear – if Finns choose to be miserable that's their business, I say – but if an oily-fish canning company wants to pay me good money to find out, why should I care? Maybe Finns are miserable because they eat a lot of oily fish. It would certainly make me miserable having to eat a lot of oily fish, that's for sure. But I digress. The reason I am writing to you is because the last time I was in Finland I never moved out of Helsinki, whereas this time I need to get around the country. As I would prefer to do this by air whenever possible I was wondering if Finnair operate an internal service? Perhaps you could advise me? If you do, a timetable would be very much appreciated.

At the same time, any observations you may have on why you Finns are so miserable – apart from having to eat oily fish – would be most welcome.

Yours sincerely

T Ravenscroft (Mr)

The Elms
Wenter Road
New Mills
High Peak
Derbyshire

Finnair
14 Clifford Street   7th May
LONDON
W1X 1RD

Dear Finnair

Thank you for the copy of 'Finnair Travel Info & Timetable'
which was most welcome – despite the fact that it smelled of
oily fish. I suppose the Finn who put it in the envelope had
eaten oily fish for his lunch, and I'm sure I don't have to tell
you how difficult it is to get rid of the smell of oily fish once
you get it on your hands.

You didn't respond to my request for your observations on
why the Finns are so miserable – but, thinking about it, I
suppose that to do otherwise would have been a contradiction
of this fact, whereas to ignore it only confirms the need for
my study. For this I thank you.

Yours faithfully

T Ravenscroft (Mr)

The Elms
Wenter Road
New Mills
High Peak
Derbyshire

Air Lanka
22 Regent Street
LONDON
SW1Y 4QD

2nd May

Dear Air Lanka

I will be flying to Sri Lanka with your airline in August, and am wondering if I will be able to get a decent cup of tea on your aeroplane, because if not I'll pop a couple of Co-op 99 tea bags in my hand baggage, so that one of your cabin staff will be able to brew me a cup. Naturally I will be taking a supply of Co-op 99 tea bags with me to your country, as, unlike countries like India and Ceylon, I suppose Sri Lanka is like all the other Mediterranean islands I have been to, and doesn't have any tea of its own.

Perhaps you would be good enough to advise me?

Yours faithfully

T Ravenscroft (Mr)

AIRLANKA LIMITED

22 REGENT STREET, LONDON SW1Y 4QD
Tel: 071-930 2099 (Administration)   071-930 4688 (Reservations)
Tel: 071- 930 3766 (Cargo)
Fax: 071-930 5626   Telex: 269171 LANKA G

26 May
Mr. T. Ravenscroft,
The Elms
Wenter Road
New Mills
High Peak
Derbyshire

Dear Mr. Ravenscroft,

Thank you for your recent letter regarding your forthcoming
flights to Sri Lanka. In answer to your query regarding tea
on our flights, I would like to assure you that we only use
pure Ceylon Tea. You seem to have not realised that Sri lanka
is the new name for Ceylon and as you know Sri Lanka is one
of the world's major producer of fine teas. So wether on our
flights or during your stay in Sri Lanka, you should not have
any need to bring your own tea.

I hope this clarifies your querie, and may I take this
oportunity to wish you a good flight and a happy holiday.

Yours sincerely

Hasan Scarr
Sales representative

A Member of

IATA

Incorporated in Sri Lanka with limited liability

The Elms
Wenter Road
New Mills
High Peak
Derbyshire

Hasan Scarr
Air Lanka Ltd   31st May
22 Regent Street
LONDON
SW1Y 4QD

Dear Hasan Scarr

Thank you for your letter of 26th May.

You are wrong, I didn't know that Sri Lanka produces tea – I'd always thought it was made at the Co-op or Sainsbury's. On learning this I was of course quite relieved, although I am more than a little concerned about your use of the word 'fine' to describe your tea. Qantas Airways used the word 'fine' when describing their Australian wine, and if the Sri Lankan idea of what constitutes fine is anything like the Australian one your tea will be so tannic that it could remove paint at twenty paces! Perhaps you could send me a sample of your tea so that I might judge for myself whether or not it is drinkable?

As you suspected, I didn't realise that Sri Lanka was once Ceylon, so thanks for the history lesson. I sincerely hope that it is still in the Mediterranean!

I have always believed in repaying a kindness with a kindness, so in return for the history lesson I offer you a spelling lesson. Wether is spelt weather, querie is spelt query (you had it right the first time), oportunity is spelt opportunity, and Hasan is spelt Hassan.

Looking forward to receiving the sample of your tea.
Yours sincerely

T Ravenscroft (Mr)

The Elms
Wenter Road
New Mills
High Peak
Derbyshire

Cathay Pacific Airways Ltd
52 Berkeley Street   7th May
LONDON
W1X 5FP

Dear Cathay Pacific Airways

I wish to complain most strongly about an incident which
occurred on a recent flight I made with your airline from Hong
Kong to London.

In the late evening, a few minutes after the cabin lights had been
dimmed, the young couple seated next to me started making
love. When I say 'making love' I don't mean making love in the
old-fashioned sense of kissing and canoodling, but in the
modern sense – in other words this was full in-flight fornicating.

You might think that possibly the young couple thought that
I was asleep, and therefore wouldn't notice, but nothing
could be further from the truth, indeed the young lady asked
me to hold her handbag. To say I was shocked would be
putting it mildly; in fact I was so disturbed by the experience
that I couldn't sleep for the rest of the journey from thinking
about it.

I didn't report the incident at the time, nor did I make any
attempt to register my disapproval to the couple, as the young
man was the 'physical' type, and I know better than to tangle
with a man when he is sexually aroused.

Before I decide what to do about the incident I would like to
hear your views on the advisability or otherwise of aeroplanes

dimming their cabin lights during night flights, as I doubt very much that the couple would have dared to do what they did had the lights remained on. Or at least not with such abandon. Personally, in view of what happened, and what I was forced to witness, I would prefer it if all the lights remained on throughout the journey, but maybe there are technical reasons why this isn't possible?

I await your reply.

Yours faithfully

T Ravenscroft (Mr)

CATHAY PACIFIC ✈

CATHAY PACIFIC AIRWAYS LIMITED
7, Apple Tree Yard, Duke of York Street,
London SW1Y 6LD.

Customer
Relations: 071-747 7001
Telex: 918120 Cathex G.
Facsimile No: 071-839 5070
Direct Line:

13th May

Mr. T. Ravenscroft,
The Elms
Wenter Road
New Mills
High Peak
Derbyshire

Dear Mr. Ravenscroft,

Thank you for your letter of 7th May regarding your recent flight with Cathay Pacific from Hong Kong to London.

We would very much like to investigate what happened with the cabin crew concerned but unfortunately you do not mention your date of travel.

Would you be so kind as to let us know when you flew? We look forward to hearing from you further and, in the meantime, regret that you have been so disturbed.

Yours sincerely,

for and on behalf of
CATHAY PACIFIC AIRWAYS LTD
C.M. Boylan (Mrs)
Customer Relations Officer

Recycled

The Elms
Wenter Road
New Mills
High Peak
Derbyshire

C.M.Boylan (Mrs)
Cathay Pacific Airways Ltd   17th May
52 Berkeley Street
LONDON
W1X 5FP

Dear Mrs Boylan

Thank you for the prompt reply to my recent letter.

I am afraid, with your statement 'We would very much like to investigate what happened with the cabin crew concerned', that you must have misunderstood me. I wasn't suggesting that it was the members of the cabin crew who were indulging in in-flight fornication! Nothing could be further from the truth. In fact I have nothing but the highest praise for your cabin crew, all of whose behaviour was exemplary throughout the entire journey. Granted I did at one stage notice the Captain and a stewardess disappear for ten minutes into the cubbyhole where you store the meals, but, although such an occurrence could give rise to suspicions of impropriety by those on the lookout for mischief, I personally prefer to think that whatever they were doing there was official business – despite my hearing what sounded very much like the pop of a champagne cork, and the Captain emerging from the cubbyhole a little breathless and dishevelled.

No, the couple in question were passengers, a young couple from Dagenham according to the label on their hand baggage – she very possibly being one of the Dagenham Girl Pipers from the way she was behaving with intimate parts of his body!

I am sure you will be glad to know that I have now got over the experience and am no longer disturbed.

You didn't say anything in your letter regarding my point that it might not be a bad idea if all the cabin lights remained on during the entire flight. I feel quite strongly about this one and I really would appreciate Cathay Pacific's observations, as I may very well pursue the matter with the Civil Aviation Authorities.

Yours sincerely

T Ravenscroft (Mr)

The Elms
Wenter Road
New Mills
High Peak
Derbyshire

Korean Air
66/68 Piccadilly   6th May
LONDON
W1V 0HJ

Dear Korean Air

In a few weeks' time I will be travelling to Seoul with your airline, and would be grateful for some pre-flight information from you.

As I will be in Korea for up to a month I intend taking my inflatable rubber woman with me (my Seoul mate, ha ha!). I had intended to pack it in my suitcase but it struck me that it is rather a long flight to Korea, and I might need some comfort during the journey, so would it be in order for me to carry it in my hand baggage?

Looking forward to hearing from you.

Yours faithfully

T Ravenscroft (Mr)

KOREAN AIR 대 한 항 공

U.K & IRELAND: 66/68 PICCADILLY LONDON W1V OHJ
TEL:(071)495-0077/(071)495-3377/(071)495-2299, FAX:(071)495-1616

10th May

Mr. T. Ravenscroft,
The Elms
Wenter Road
New Mills
High Peak
Derbyshire

Dear Mr. Ravenscroft,

Thank you for your letter dated 4 May inquiring about our policy concerning the acceptability of certain 'carry-on' items of baggage.

I would recommend that you do not attempt to travel with your prosthetic device in order to avoid possible embarrassment to yourself and contravention of Korean morality laws.

Yours sincerely,

CATHAY PACIFIC AIRWAYS LTD
M. Scorah
Asst.Manager Reservations/Ticketing
KOREAN AIR

M. Scorah
Korean Air
66/68 Piccadilly
LONDON
W1V 0HJ

The Elms
Wenter Road
New Mills
High Peak
Derbyshire

16th May

Dear M. Scorah

Reference your letter of 10th May.

How dare you! My inflatable rubber woman is not a prosthetic device. For your information a prosthetic device is something which makes up for certain deficiencies, such as false teeth or an artificial leg. You are implying that I am deficient of a woman, and this I am most certainly not, as my lovely wife can testify.

My inflatable rubber woman – which, incidentally, has no 'working parts' – is used simply to comfort me, much as a teddy bear or a piece of material from its first dressing gown would comfort a child. I simply blow up Big Bertha and sit her on my knee for half an hour or so. How this could cause embarrassment to anyone is quite beyond me! It is possible someone might get the wrong idea if we hit a bit of turbulence, but that is hardly my fault, is it?

As far as Korean morals are concerned, I think the Koreans proved fairly conclusively in the Korean War that they don't have any morals whatsoever, so the less said about that subject the better.

I am on the verge of flying to Korea with another airline!

Yours sincerely

T Ravenscroft (Mr)

The Elms
Wenter Road
New Mills
High Peak
Derbyshire

Yemenia Yemen Airways
52 Stratton Street
LONDON
W1X 5FF

16th May

Dear Yemenia Yemen Airways

I am considering taking a holiday in the Republic of Yemen in a few weeks' time, and if I decide in the affirmative I will be travelling with your airline.

However, something I read in a travel brochure has given me some cause for concern. Apparently it is the practice over there to use the right hand only to shake hands or pass things with, and also to eat with. This puts me at a distinct disadvantage because I do not possess a right hand. (I lost it in a lawnmower.) Does this mean that I would be unable to shake hands or pass anything, or, more importantly, eat anything, whilst I am in the Yemen? Because, quite frankly, I don't much care for the idea of going without food and not passing anything for two weeks, even if the food over there is pretty dire.

I don't know what function the left hand fulfils in Yemeni life but on the face of it it appears to be pretty redundant. A friend informs me that it is used solely to wipe one's bottom with, but I must say I find this hard to believe, as I use my left hand to wipe my bottom with and I am no more Yemeni than the Queen of England.

Could my friend possibly be correct? If so, do you think it possible that the authorities might give me some special dispensation to use my left hand? My friend says that the left hand is considered to be unclean, but personally I would rather eat unclean food than no food at all, even if it is only goat stew. I really would like to visit the Republic of Yemen, so perhaps you can help me here?

Yours faithfully

T Ravenscroft (Mr)

Yemenia ✈ اليمنية
Yemen Airways
الخطوط الجوية اليمنية

52 STRATTON STREET, LONDON W1X 5FF. UNITED KINGDOM.
TEL: 071-491 7186 (Res/Ticketing) 071-409 2171 (Administration).
FAX: 071-355 3062 TELEX: 269292 YEMAIR G. SITA: LONZQIY

23rd May

REF: LONIY803

Mr. T. Ravenscroft,
The Elms
Wenter Road
New Mills
High Peak
Derbyshire

Dear Mr. Ravenscroft,

Thank you for your letter regarding your consideration to take a holiday to Yemen.

Let me assure you Sir that you will have no worries whatsoever in regards in what you have mentioned in your letter. However we can whish you a happy time should you decide to chose to go to Yemen anytime. You are more than welcome in our country.

Should you require any further assistance please do not hesitate to contact me.

Yours sincerely,

Ali Ibrahim Jawee
Area Manager for UK & Ire

More than a choice   اكــثــر مــن إخــتــيـار

The Elms
Wenter Road
New Mills
High Peak
Derbyshire

Ali Ibrahim Jawee
Yemenia Yemen Airways   31st May
52 Stratton Street
LONDON
W1X 5FF

Dear Ali Ibrahim Jawee

Thank you for your letter of 24th May.

Since writing to you I have learned that for the last four weeks there has been a civil war raging in the Republic of Yemen. I do think you might have mentioned it! I certainly won't look out of place with my right hand missing, will I, as lots of Yemenis will no doubt be losing their right hands, along with various other parts of their bodies. However, as you must have been aware that there was a war going on when you wrote to me, and were still able to 'whish me a happy time in Yemen anytime', it is obvious that you feel that holidaymakers aren't in any danger, so I will be coming in early July.

I must say how very apt the Yemenia Yemen Airways motto 'More than a choice' is. It absolutely typifies what you are about, because I've flown with dozens of airlines in my time but it's certainly the first time I've ever been offered the choice of a holiday plus a war!

Despite your confidence that I won't come to any harm, I do think it would be less than prudent of me if I were not to take the precaution of wearing bulletproof casual and beachwear during my stay with you. Will these items be readily available in the Yemen or will I have to bring them with me?

Yours sincerely

T Ravenscroft (Mr)

The Elms
Wenter Road
New Mills
High Peak
Derbyshire

Egyptair
Walmar House   3rd May
296 Regent Street
LONDON
W1R 6PH

Dear Egyptair

Congratulations! I am delighted to inform you that your airline has won the inaugural New Mills Airline Passenger Club Award.

The contest was a particularly exciting and close-run thing this year. Right up until the last minute it was between Egyptair and Air 2000, the latter receiving very high marks for its lasagne from me, but very low marks for its lasagne from everyone else, thus tipping the balance in your favour. A very close third was Air UK for its stewardesses' uniforms.

What finally swayed the judges in your favour was an incident which happened on a flight with Egyptair from London to Cairo. Apparently the ten-year-old son of a New Mills Airline Passenger Club member was slapped quite viciously round the face by one of your stewardesses, whilst he was having a tantrum, with the result that the child thoroughly behaved himself for the remainder of the flight, and well into the holiday. Although I say 'whilst he was having a tantrum', it isn't exactly clear whether the stewardess (it was the one with the moustache by the way) slapped the boy round the face to bring him out of his tantrum, or caused him to have a tantrum by slapping him round the face. However it doesn't really matter either way, because according to the father of the boy, who can be a bit of a swine to say the least, the brat deserved a slap round the face whether he was having a tantrum or not.

The award, which does not carry any financial reward, consists of a trophy depicting a scale model Boeing 767 airliner in the Egyptair livery, touching down on a life-size concrete model of a piece of lost luggage, with a plaque inscribed 'Egyptair – Airline of the Year 2006'. And most elegant it is too.

Will you please therefore advise me what to do with this prestigious trophy, regarding delivery to you?

Yours faithfully

T Ravenscroft (Mr)
Hon Sec New Mills Airline Passenger Club